God's
Divine Instructions To End Time Saints

God's Divine Instructions To End Time Saints

Jesus Christ is coming again

❧

AELTON SIMMONS

Copyright © 2022 by Aelton Simmons.

All rights reserved. No part of this publication may be reproduced, distributed, or transmitted in any form or by any means, including photocopying, recording, or other electronic or mechanical methods, without the prior written permission of the author, except in the case of brief quotations embodied in critical reviews and certain other noncommercial uses permitted by copyright law.

All scripture quotations, unless otherwise specified, are from the King James Version of the Holy Bible.

Printed in the United States of America

ISBN 978-1-64133-689-5 (paperback)

LCCN: 2022900965

Inspirational

MainSpring Books
5901 W. Century Blvd
Suite 750
Los Angeles, CA, US, 90045
www.mainspringbooks.com

FOR MORE INFORMATION, PLEASE CONTACT:

A. C. Simmons
962 Kingswood Estate
Pine Bluff, AR 71613
870-329-0956

Contents

Lesson 1	Are you Saved?	3
Lesson 2	God Reveals To His Servants Things To Come	9
Lesson 3	Things Saints Should Do	15
Lesson 4	Things God has done, is doing, and shall do	25
Lesson 5	Major Events That Will Happen In The Last Days	37
Lesson 6	The Physical Creation	103
Lesson 7	Earthquakes, Mudslides, Volcanic Eruptions, and Other Natural Catastrophes	123
Lesson 8	Strange Occurrences In Outer Space	151
Lesson 9	Blind to the Signs	159
Lesson 10	What Religions Will Be Doing Part. 1	169
Lesson 11	What Religions Will Be Doing Part. 2	189
Lesson 12	What Nations Will Be Doing Part. 1	209
Lesson 13	What Nations Will Be Doing Part. 2	225
Lesson 14	The Great Tribulation Period	237
Lesson 15	The Millennium	249
Lesson 16	Eternity Future	259
Lesson 17	Overview of God's dealings with mankind	265

(1ˢᵗ Peter. 4:7) ⁷But **the end of all things is at hand**: be ye therefore sober, and watch unto prayer.

(Revelation. 1:3) ³Blessed is he that readeth, and they that hear the words of this prophecy, and keep those things which are written therein: **for the time is at hand**.

Are you Saved?

Are you saved?

(John.1:12) 12. But as many as received him, to them gave he power to become the sons of God, even to them that believe on his name:

Are you saved? Are you a born again Child of God? If you are not a Christian; or if you are not sure you are a Christian, you need to pray the prayer below. Praying the prayer below, and meaning it from your heart will make you a Christian. Once you finish praying this prayer, you will become a child of God, and you will always be a child of God. If you pray it today, write today's date down and forever remember it as the date you were born again (became a Christian).

Dear God in heaven I do believe that Jesus Christ is Your only begotten Son who died on the Cross for the sins of the world, and three days later You raised Him from the dead. I now ask You to forgive me of my sins and for Jesus to come into my heart and be my Lord and Savior. You promised if I believe and confess; I will be saved. Because I am now believing and confessing; You are now saving me and making me Your child. Thank you Father, in Jesus name, amen.

*(Romans.10:9-10,13) 9. That if thou shalt **confess** with thy mouth the Lord Jesus, and shalt **believe** in thine heart that God hath raised him from the dead, thou shalt be saved. 10. For with the heart man **believeth** unto righteousness; and with the mouth **confession** is made unto salvation. 13. For whosoever shall call upon the name of the Lord shall be saved.*

Things that happen to a person once they become saved

1. All their sins are forgiven (Colossians.2:13).

2. All their sins are washed away by the blood of Jesus Christ (Revelation.1:5; 1st Corinthians.6:11).

3. All their sins are forever forgotten about by God (Hebrews.8:12).

4. Their spirit is instantly transformed from being in the image of the devil into being in the image of Jesus Christ. This is called being born again (2nd Corinthians.5:17).

5. The Holy Spirit comes to live in their heart never to leave them (John.14:17; Romans.8:9).

6. They instantly and forever become a child of God (Romans.6:18; Galatians.3:26-27).

7. They are instantly translated into the body of Christ which is the family of God. This is called being baptized into the body of Christ (1st Corinthians.12:13; Galatians.3:27).

8. They are sealed into the body of Christ until the day of redemption (Ephesians.4:30).

9. They instantly receive eternal everlasting life (John.10:28-29).

10. Their eternal destination is changed from hell and the lake of fire into spending eternity with Jesus Christ (Jude.1:23; Revelation.20:15).

11. They become a joint heir with Jesus Christ (Romans.8:16-17).

12. They are babes in Christ and must grow spiritually by growing in the written Word of God (1st Peter.2:2; 2nd Peter,3:18).

13. So much, much more (1st Corinthians.2:9-11).

The consequences of not being saved and thus not having your name written down in the Lamb's book of life

(Revelation.20:11-16) 11. And I saw a great white throne, and him that sat on it, from whose face the earth and the heaven fled away; and there was found no place for them. 12. And I saw the dead, small and great, stand before God; and the books were opened: and another book was opened, which is the book of life: and the dead were judged out of those things which were written in the books, according to their works. 13. And the sea gave up the dead which were in it; and death and hell delivered up the dead which were in them: and they were judged every man according to their works. 14. And death and hell were cast into the lake of fire. This is the second death. 15. **<u>And whosoever was not found written in the book of life was cast into the lake of fire</u>**.

When I think about what God the Father through His Son the Lord Jesus Christ has delivered me from, and delivered me to; I rejoice with joy unspeakable and full of glory. I daily strive to increase in my love for God, and increase in showing my love to Him. I worship Him, live for Him, and serve Him with all my heart, soul, and body.

Are you appreciative to God for all He has done? Do you daily strive to increase in showing your love and appreciation to God? If you love Him as you should, you will live for Him, and you will serve Him with all that is within you. You will tell everyone you can about His goodness, and about the salvation He offers.

God Reveals To His Servants Things To Come

They dreamed about them, they prophesied about them, and they wrote about them. God through the prophets, seers, and Holy Ghost filled prognosticators of ancient times revealed many of the horrific events which will transpire at the end of days. Oh how sad it would be to have these prophetic writings available to us; but, we not know of them, not understand them, and not realize they are transpiring in our world today.

It is now time for all saints to become wise, educated, and informed concerning end time events as revealed by the Holy written Word of God. God placed these things in His written Word because He wanted His children to know about them, and to prepare themselves for the soon return of Jesus Christ.

God reveals to His servants things to come

> *(Amos.3:7)* 7. Surely the Lord God will do nothing, but **he revealeth his secret unto his servants** the prophets.

> *(Isaiah.42:9)* 9. Behold, the former things are come to pass, and new things do I declare: **before they spring forth I tell you of them**

> *(Isaiah.46:10)* 10. **Declaring the end from the beginning**, and from ancient times the things that are not yet done, saying, My counsel shall stand, and I will do all my pleasure:

God in His written Word has revealed Himself, His love, His holiness, His grace, and His eternal plan and purpose. He wants saints to know who He is and what He is doing. He also wants saints to know how they are to live in order to line up with His eternal plan and purpose.

"God's Divine Instructions to End Time Saints" will help reveal to you what God has done, is doing, and is going to do. It will help reveal to you how close we are to the soon return of Jesus Christ, and what you should do in light of His soon return.

1. **God reveals things to come to His saints because He wants them to know what He is going to do.**

   > *(John.16:13)* ¹³ Howbeit when he, the Spirit of truth, is come, he will guide you into all truth: for he shall not speak of himself; but whatsoever he shall hear, that shall he speak: and **he will show you things to come**.

Saints must advance to levels where we can hear God revealing to us things to come in this world, in our lives, and in the lives of others. We need to hear God speaking through His written Word, through His Holy Spirit in us, and through our circumstances. Do not just notice what's going on around you; seek to hear what God is saying to you through the things going on around You. God is up to something in your circumstances; and you need to let Him reveal to you what He is doing, and what He is saying.

2. **God reveals things to come to His saints because He wants them to be ready and prepared for what's about to happen in their lives and in this world.**

   *(Luke.21:34) ³⁴And take heed to yourselves, lest at any time your hearts be overcharged with surfeiting, and drunkenness, and cares of this life, **and so that day come upon you unawares***

Saints must allow God to prepare them for things to come in this world, in our lives, and in the lives of others. Because of the horrendous things which are about to happen, we need warnings and instructions from God on what to do to escape harm and loss. Daily ask God for the spirit of wisdom, revelation, and instruction.

3. **God reveals things to come to His saints because He does not want them to be filled with worry doubt and fear.**

   *(Matthew.24:6) ⁶And ye shall hear of wars and rumours of wars: **see that ye be not troubled**: for all these things must come to pass, but the end is not yet.*

End time events of epic proportions are about to transpire on earth and in our lives. God knows what's about to happen; thus He is seeking to warn us and prepare us so we will walk in faith; not in fear. Because of the warnings God is giving; saints must daily strive to increase, improve, and intensify their faith so they can trust Him regardless of what's going on around them. Pray constantly, study the Word daily, and worship God in everything; so your faith will constantly increase in Him.

4. **God reveals things to come to His saints because He wants them to know that the eternal plans and purposes He has for man centers**

around His love for man, and the redemptive work of His Son Jesus Christ on the Cross.

> (John.5:39) ³⁹*Search the scriptures; for in them ye think ye have eternal life: and* **they are they which testify of me**.

> (Revelation.19:10) ¹⁰*And I fell at his feet to worship him. And he said unto me, See thou do it not: I am thy fellowservant, and of thy brethren that have the testimony of Jesus: worship God:* **for the testimony of Jesus is the spirit of prophecy**.

Do the things you experience and go through draw you to Jesus Christ? Do the things you go through cause you to increase in realizing how mush God loves you? Do you realize God is preparing you to spend eternity with Him? Always be conscience of the fact that God is doing things in you and in your life to reveal His love to you; and to prepare you to spend eternity with Him. Salvation is a love thing and an eternal thing.

5. **God reveals things to come to His saints because He wants them to believe in Him and in what He says.**

   > (John.14:29) ²⁹*And now I have told you* **before it come to pass, that, when it is come to pass, ye might believe**.

Knowing that only God can reveal the events of the future with such accuracy as the Holy Bible does, should cause you to believe in Him and in the things He says. The more end time events transpire, the more your belief should increase.

6. **God reveals things to come to His saints because He wants them to look to Him in all things.**

   > (Jeremiah.33:2-3) ²*Thus saith the LORD the maker thereof, the LORD that formed it, to establish it; the LORD is his name;* **3Call unto me, and I will answer thee, and show thee great and mighty things, which thou knowest not**.

Because of things which are about to transpire on earth and in the lives of people; Saints and people will realize no one can help them but God. However; God's help comes only through Jesus Christ. Saints must learn to depend on Jesus for everything and in everything. We must not depend on our jobs, people, or ourselves. We must look to God through Jesus Christ as He works through jobs, people, and other things.

7. **God reveals things to come to His saints because He wants to motivate them to study His written Word.**

   (Daniel.9:2) ²In the first year of his reign I Daniel understood by books the number of the years, whereof the word of the LORD came to Jeremiah the prophet, that he would accomplish seventy years in the desolations of Jerusalem.

There are too many awesome benefits, blessings, and bonuses that come from reading, studying, and meditating on the Word for saints to neglect the Word. Having a desire of wanting to know what's about to transpire on this planet, and in our lives should motivate saints to daily study the Word. Studying the Word increases your faith, and gives you wisdom, knowledge, and instructions on what to do.

8. **God reveals things to come to His saints because He wants saints to be ready for the soon return of Jesus Christ by living righteous, and doing the works Jesus Christ would have them do.**

   (1ˢᵗ Peter.4:7) ⁷But the end of all things is at hand: **<u>be ye therefore sober, and watch unto prayer</u>**.

Are you ready for the soon return of Jesus Christ? Are you living righteous? Are you performing your works of service every time you are supposed to perform them? Momma use to say; "boy, don't let the Lord come and catch you with your works undone". Momma was right.

9. **God reveals things to come to His saints because He wants saints to witness to people about the soon return of Jesus Christ, and tell them they need to accept Jesus Christ as their Lord and Savior now.**

   (Matthew.3:7-8) ⁷But when he saw many of the Pharisees and Sadducees come to his baptism, he said unto them, O generation of vipers, <u>**who hath warned you to flee from the wrath to come?**</u> *⁸Bring forth therefore fruits meet for repentance:*

Who have you told about Jesus lately? Who have you invited to accept Jesus Christ as their Lord and Savior lately? Hell is too hot, and eternity is too long, for you to allow people to go to hell without first telling them about Jesus Christ and the salvation He offers to all? Never be ashamed or afraid to ask people to receive Jesus Christ as Lord and Savior.

Things Saints Should Do

Things saints should do

1. **Be sure you are saved**

    (2nd Corinthians.13:5) [5]*Examine yourselves, whether ye be in the faith; prove your own selves. Know ye not your own selves, how that Jesus Christ is in you, except ye be reprobates?*

2. **Love God supremely**

    (Matthew.22:37-38) [37]*Jesus said unto him, Thou shalt love the Lord thy God with all thy heart, and with all thy soul, and with all thy mind.* [38]*This is the first and great commandment.*

3. **Always love others as you love yourself**

    (Matthew.22:39) [39]*And the second is like unto it, Thou shalt love thy neighbour as thyself.*

4. **Always put God first**

    (Matthew.6:33-34) [33]*But seek ye first the kingdom of God, and his righteousness; and all these things shall be added unto you.* [34]*Take therefore no thought for the morrow: for the morrow shall take thought for the things of itself. Sufficient unto the day is the evil thereof.*

5. **Obey God over men and government**

    (Acts.5:29) [29]*Then Peter and the other apostles answered and said, We ought to obey God rather than men.*

6. **Constantly increase in the knowledge of God**

    (Daniel.11:32) ³²And such as do wickedly against the covenant shall he corrupt by flatteries: but the people that do know their God shall be strong, and do exploits.

7. **Give yourself to constant prayer**

    (1ˢᵗ Thessalonians.5:17) ¹⁷Pray without ceasing.

> Saints can not afford to fall short of being all God wants them to be; and doing all God wants them to do. When He reveals what to do; get busy doing it by the power of the Holy Ghost.

8. **Constantly worship and praise God**

    (Psalm.34:1-3) ¹ I will bless the LORD at all times: his praise shall continually be in my mouth. ² My soul shall make her boast in the LORD: the humble shall hear thereof, and be glad. ³ O magnify the LORD with me, and let us exalt his name together.

9. **Constantly witness to sinners inviting them to become saved**

    (Mark.16:15-16) ¹⁵And he said unto them, Go ye into all the world, and preach the gospel to every creature. ¹⁶He that believeth and is baptized shall be saved; but he that believeth not shall be damned.

10. **Learn to hear the voice of God in your spirit**

    (John.10:27) ²⁷My sheep hear my voice, and I know them, and they follow me

11. Do not allow your heart to be troubled.

(Matthew.24:6) ⁶And ye shall hear of wars and rumours of wars: see that ye be not troubled: for all these things must come to pass, but the end is not yet.

12. Keep your mind stayed on God

(Isaiah.26:3-4) ³Thou wilt keep him in perfect peace, whose mind is stayed on thee: because he trusteth in thee. ⁴Trust ye in the LORD for ever: for in the LORD JEHOVAH is everlasting strength:

13. Remember greater is He that is in you than He that is in the world

(1ˢᵗ John.4:4) ⁴Ye are of God, little children, and have overcome them: because greater is he that is in you, than he that is in the world.

14. Learn to overcome evil with Good

(Romans.12:21) ²¹Be not overcome of evil, but overcome evil with good.

15. Learn to endure suffering

(Philippiand.1:29) ²⁹For unto you it is given in the behalf of Christ, not only to believe on him, but also to suffer for his sake;

16. Remember God is your supplier

(Philippians.4:19) ¹⁹But my God shall supply all your need according to his riches in glory by Christ Jesus.

17. Remember God is your protector

(Psalms.91:5-12) ⁵ *Thou shalt not be afraid for the terror by night; nor for the arrow that flieth by day;⁶ Nor for the pestilence that walketh in darkness; nor for the destruction that wasteth at noonday.⁷ A thousand shall fall at thy side, and ten thousand at thy right hand; but it shall not come nigh thee.⁸ Only with thine eyes shalt thou behold and see the reward of the wicked.⁹ Because thou hast made the LORD, which is my refuge, even the most High, thy habitation;¹⁰ There shall no evil befall thee, neither shall any plague come nigh thy dwelling.¹¹ For he shall give his angels charge over thee, to keep thee in all thy ways.*

18. Increase in operating in the gifts of the Spirit

*(1ˢᵗ Corinthians.12:7-11) ⁷But the manifestation of the Spirit is given to every man to profit withal. ⁸For to one is given by the Spirit the **word of wisdom**; to another **the word of knowledge** by the same Spirit; ⁹To another **faith** by the same Spirit; to another the gifts of **healing** by the same Spirit; ¹⁰To another the **working of miracles**; to another **prophecy**; to another **discerning of spirits**; to another divers kinds of **tongues**; to another the **interpretation of tongues**: ¹¹But all these worketh that one and the selfsame Spirit, dividing to every man severally as he will.*

19. Have on the whole armor of God

*(Ephesians.6:13-18) ¹³Wherefore take unto you the whole armour of God, that ye may be able to withstand in the evil day, and having done all, to stand. ¹⁴Stand therefore, having your loins girt about with **truth**, and having on the breastplate of **righteousness**; ¹⁵And your feet shod with the preparation of **the gospel of peace**; ¹⁶Above all, taking **the shield of faith**, wherewith ye shall be able to quench all the fiery darts of the wicked. ¹⁷And take the **helmet of salvation**, and the sword of the Spirit, which is **the word of God**: 18Praying always*

with all prayer and supplication in the Spirit, and watching thereunto with all perseverance and supplication for all saints;

20. Know the weapons of your warfare

(2nd Corinthians.10:4-6) ^{3}For though we walk in the flesh, we do not war after the flesh: ^{4}(For the weapons of our warfare are not carnal, but mighty through God to the pulling down of strong holds;) ^{5}Casting down imaginations, and every high thing that exalteth itself against the knowledge of God, and bringing into captivity every thought to the obedience of Christ; ^{6}And having in a readiness to revenge all disobedience, when your obedience is fulfilled.

21. Use the word of your testimony

(Revelation.12:11) ^{11}And they overcame him by the blood of the Lamb, and by the word of their testimony; and they loved not their lives unto the death. (Mark.11:22-23) ^{22}And Jesus answering saith unto them, Have faith in God. ^{23}For verily I say unto you, That whosoever shall say unto this mountain, Be thou removed, and be thou cast into the sea; and shall not doubt in his heart, but shall believe that those things which he saith shall come to pass; he shall have whatsoever he saith

22. Live in the fruit of the spirit

*(Galatians.5:22-23) ^{22}But the fruit of the Spirit is **love**, **joy**, **peace**, **longsuffering**, **gentleness**, **goodness**, **faith**, ^{23}**Meekness**, **temperance**: against such there is no law.*

23. Increase in perfecting your faith

(Romans.10:17) ^{17}So then faith cometh by hearing, and hearing by the word of God.

> **Saints have been given too much Power for us to live Powerless lives. Have you learned to live by the Power of God?**

(Jude.1:20) [20]*But ye, beloved, building up yourselves on your most holy faith, praying in the Holy Ghost,*

24. Learn not to deny the power of God and stay away from those who do

(2nd Timothy.3:5) [5]*Having a form of godliness, but denying the power thereof: from such turn away.*

25. Learn to daily live by the Power of God

(1st Corinthians.4:20) [20]*For the kingdom of God is not in word, but in power.*

26. Learn to use the power of binding and loosening

(Matthew.16:19) [19]*And I will give unto thee the keys of the kingdom of heaven: and whatsoever thou shalt bind on earth shall be bound in heaven: and whatsoever thou shalt loose on earth shall be loosed in heaven (Matthew.18:18)* [18]*Verily I say unto you, Whatsoever ye shall bind on earth shall be bound in heaven: and whatsoever ye shall loose on earth shall be loosed in heaven.*

27. Learn the power of the prayer of agreement

[19]*Again I say unto you, That if two of you shall agree on earth as touching any thing that they shall ask, it shall be done for them of my Father which is in heaven.* [20]*For where two or three are gathered together in my name, there am I in the midst of them.*

28. Continue serving God

(2nd Timothy.4:5) [5]*But watch thou in all things, endure afflictions, do the work of an evangelist, make full proof of thy ministry*

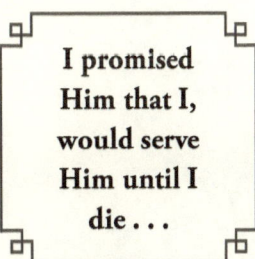

I promised Him that I, would serve Him until I die . . .

29. **Live a righteous lifestyle**

Proverbs.14:34) ³⁴Righteousness exalteth a nation: but sin is a reproach to any people

30. **Never take the mark of the beast**

(Revelation.14:9-11) ⁹And the third angel followed them, saying with a loud voice, If any man worship the beast and his image, and receive his mark in his forehead, or in his hand, ¹⁰The same shall drink of the wine of the wrath of God, which is poured out without mixture into the cup of his indignation; and he shall be tormented with fire and brimstone in the presence of the holy angels, and in the presence of the Lamb: ¹¹And the smoke of their torment ascendeth up for ever and ever: and they have no rest day nor night, who worship the beast and his image, and whosoever receiveth the mark of his name.

Victory of the saints

I believe God will Rapture the church before the Tribulation Period; however, before the Rapture occurs, many hideous, horrendous, and horrifying things will happen. During the Tribulation Period; the worst things that has ever happened in human history will happen. If God does not Rapture saints before the Tribulation Period, saints will endure it. However, regardless of which time period we find ourselves in, saints can live in victory because:

A. We are saved (1st John.5:4-5).

B. We have God with us (*Hebrews 13:5*).

C. We have God protecting us (*Psalm 61:3, Psalm 91:10-12*).

D. We have God providing for us (*Philippians 4:19*).

E. We have God and His power in us through the Holy Ghost (*Acts 1:8*).

F. We have the weapons of our warfare (*2nd Corinthians 10:4-6*).

G. We have the whole armor of God (*Ephesians 6:10-18*).

H. We have the gifts of the Spirit (*1st Corinthians 12:4-11*).

I. We have the fruit of the Spirit (*Galatians 5:22-23*).

J. We have ministry gifts (*Ephesians 4:11-16*).

K. We have the word of our testimony (*Revelation 12:11*).

L. We have the blood of the Lamb (*Revelation 12:11*).

M. We have the angels of God ministering to us (*Hebrews 1:13-14, Psalm 91:10-12*).

N. We are more than conquerors (*Romans 8:37*).

O. We always triumph (*2nd Corinthians 2:14*).

P. We have victory (*1st Corinthians 15:57*).

Q. We have the love of God overshadowing us (*Romans 8:38-39*).

R. We have the power of prayer (*John 14:13-14*).

S. We have so much, much more (*2nd Peter. 1:3*)

Things God has done, is doing, and shall do from eternity past to eternity future

How God deals with mankind From eternity past to eternity future

In this portion of our study we are going to discuss seven ways God deals with man from **Eternity Past** to **Eternity Future**. We will start with Eternity Past because He started dealing with man even before He created man (Ephesians.1:4). **While God deals with mankind in different ways; He Himself never changes**. Regardless of how He deals with man He is still love, holy, merciful, kind, the eternal Judge, Omnipotent (Almighty), Omniscient (All-knowing), Omnipresent (ever present), etc.

While we use the phrase **"Eternity Past"**; eternity has no beginning or ending. God started time for man's sake. He started it at the creation and He will end it after the Millennium. However, in God's sight, it is all a part of eternity.

The term Theologians use to describe how God deals with mankind for a certain period of time is **"Dispensations"**. *However, the divisions we are using are not dispensations as theologians classifies them. Our divisions are just an overview of how God deals with mankind. Our divisions are:*

1. **Eternity past.** The time before the physical creation.

2. **Patriarchs:** Patriarchs are chief men and women of a certain time period.

3. **The Law and the prophets:** God dealt with man through **His laws and prophets.**

4. **Grace:** "**God's un-merited favor.**" God offering men His salvation, love, and blessings although they could never deserve them, earn them, or pay for them.

5. **Tribulation Period (the time of wrath of God):** A seven-year time period when God will deal with man through His wrath, and will allow the antichrist to rule the world.

6. **Millennium:** God will deal with mankind through allowing saints to rule with Jesus Christ on earth for a Millennium (1000 years).

7. **Eternity future.** The time after the Millennium when saints will forever be with God.

Regardless of how God deals with man, He is still love, holy, just, slow to anger, full of grace, and full of compassion. **God's methods of dealing with mankind may change, but His attributes will never change.** Below is a chart of how we, and others, view what God is doing from Eternity Past to Eternity Future. **Our chart is for our study only.**

Some Theologians	Other Theologians	For our study
1. Innocence	1. Innocence	1. Eternity Past
2. Human knowledge	2. Human knowledge	2. Patriarchs
3. Human government	3. Human government	3. Law and Prophets
4. The Law and the prophets	4. Promise	4. Grace (Church age)
5. The Dispensation of grace	5. The Law and the prophets	5. Tribulation Period
6. The Tribulation Period	6. The Dispensation of grace	6. Millennium
7. The Millennium	7. The Millennium	7. Eternity Future

From eternity past to eternity future

Eternity Past	The Patriarchs Old Testament	The Law and the Prophets Old Testament	The Church Age New Testament
Creation of the third heaven where God dwells Creation of angels and all the heavenly host Fall of satan and 1/3rd of the angels God made hell and the lake of fire for the devil and his angels Preparation for creation of mankind and the redemption of mankind through Jesus Christ (see *Ephesians 1:4*)	**2000 years** Creation as found in Genesis:1-2 **Innocence** the time before men sinned **The fall** man sinned in the Garden and became sinners **Human knowledge** God now had to deal with man through human knowledge **Human Government** is established **Promise Patriarch are** (chief men and women like Noah, Abraham, Sarah, Isaac, Jacob, Job, Tamar, Joseph)	**2000 years** Moses and the Law All the events of the Old Testament from Moses to Christ **The birth** and earthly ministry of Jesus Christ. (Jesus ministered under the O.T. Law) The **death** of Jesus on the Cross **Resurrection** and **ascension** of Jesus Christ In the Holy Bible the events of the gospels are included in the New Testament; however, the New Testament really began on the day of Pentecost when the Holy Spirit came to indwell saints.	**2000 years** The Holy Spirit coming down to indwell saints All the events in the book of Acts The Epistles All of the events concerning the church **The Rapture** of the church (*1 Thessalonians 4:15-17*) Many believe that the Rapture of the church will signal the end of the Church Age of **the Dispensation of Grace** **The Church Age** is called 1. The Church Age 2. The Dispensation of Grace 3. The **Times of the Gentiles**. 4. The New Testament

Tribulation Period The time of God's wrath New Testament	**The Millennium** New Testament	**Eternity Future**
7 years	**1000 years**	**Forever and forever**
The antichrist makes a **7-year peace treaty** between Israel and her enemies the 7 seals including 1. the 4 horsemen 2. the 7 trumpets 3. The 3 woes 4. The 2 witnesses satan kicked out of heaven The beast out of the sea The beast out of the earth The mark of the beast 666 The destruction of Mystery Babylon The battle of **Armageddon** The devil bound in the bottomless pit	satan bound for 1000 years Saints ruling on earth with Jesus The devil loosed after 1000 years The devil deceives Gog and Magog to fight against the saints God sends down fire to destroy them The devil is cast into The Lake of Fire The Great White Throne Judgment seat of God Almighty The second death	The new heaven and the new earth The New Jerusalem The tree of life The river of life All of the never ending events in Eternity Future

1. **The time of the Patriarchs has passed.**

2. **The time of the laws and prophets has passed.**

3. **We are now living in the time of Grace** (also called the church age and the dispensation of grace). Many believe **the rapture of the church** will happen at the end of the time of Grace and before the Tribulation Period starts.

4. **The Tribulation Period** is the next prophetic time period after Grace.

The word "Rapture" means "being caught up". The Word "Rapture" is not found in the Holy Bible; however, it's meaning "caught up" is found in the Bible.

One day; someday, millions will vanish from off the face of the earth. While many will wonder what has happened to them; those who are familiar with Bible prophecy will know it was **the Rapture of the Church.**

> *(1st Thessalonians.4:15-18) 15For this we say unto you by the word of the Lord, that we which are alive and remain unto the coming of the Lord shall not prevent them which are asleep. 16For the Lord himself shall descend from heaven with a shout, with the voice of the archangel, and with the trump of God: and the dead in Christ shall rise first: 17Then we which are alive and remain shall be caught up together with them in the clouds, to meet the Lord in the air: and so shall we ever be with the Lord. 18Wherefore comfort one another with these words.*

While no one knows the day nor the hour when it shall occur, we do know it will happen in a moment, in an instant, and **in the twinkling of an eye.**

> *(1st Corinthians.15:51-53) 51 Behold, I show you a mystery; We shall not all sleep, but we shall all be changed, 52 In a moment, in the twinkling of an eye, at the last trump: for the trumpet shall sound, and the dead shall be raised incorruptible,*

and we shall be changed. ⁵³ *For this corruptible must put on incorruption, and this mortal must put on immortality.*

Events which will occur during the Rapture of the Church

1. The Lord Himself will descend from heaven with a shout. However; He will not touch the earth; He will stand over the earth in the clouds (Acts.1: 9-11) *⁹And when he had spoken these things, while they beheld, he was taken up; and a cloud received him out of their sight. ¹⁰And while they looked stedfastly toward heaven as he went up, behold, two men stood by them in white apparel; ¹¹Which also said, Ye men of Galilee, why stand ye gazing up into heaven? this same Jesus, which is taken up from you into heaven, shall so come in like manner as ye have seen him go into heaven.*

2. The voice of the archangel will be heard.

3. The trump of God will sound.

4. The dead in Christ (those who physically died being a Christian) will first rise from the dead. They will rise in glorified bodies.

5. Then, living saints will be changed (their bodies will be transformed into glorified bodies).

6. Then all saints shall rise to meet the Lord Jesus in the air in the clouds.

7. So shall saints ever be with the Lord.

Always remember that this will happen in a moment, in an instant, and in the twinkling of an eye. People will not see this happening, they will just notice that millions have vanished from off the earth. Many will know the Rapture (catching up of saints) has occurred, others will not know what has happened. After the vanishing of millions; chaos, confusion, and pandemonium will fill the earth; and fear will fill the hearts of men. In searching for answers to why millions have vanished, some will turn to

God, others will turn to science and men. Those who turn to God will find salvation through Jesus Christ. Those who turn to science and men will find the antichrist, and eternal damnation.

We hold to the view that **the Rapture of the church** (the church being caught up into heaven) (*1ˢᵗ Thessalonians.4:15-17*) will happen before the seven-year Tribulation Period begins; however, not all theologians hold to this view. There are three basic views concerning when the Rapture will occur. These views are centered around a seven-year time period called the Tribulation Period, and are listed below. We will discuss the Tribulation Period in greater details later in this book; however, **regardless of when the Rapture occurs; it will not change the sequence of end time events.**

Views of when the Rapture occurs?

A. **Pre-Trib**: Many believe the Rapture of the church will happen before the Tribulation Period begins. This is call the Pre-trib Rapture. (1st Thessalonians.4:15-17).

B. **Mid-trib**: Many believe the Rapture of the church will happen in the middle of the Tribulation Period. This is called Mid-trib Rapture. (Revelation.14:14-16).

C. **Post-Trib**: Many believe the Rapture of the church will happen at the end of the Tribulation Period. This is called Post-trib Rapture. (Revelation.20:5-6).

Because no one really knows when this is going to happen, everyone needs to be ready. To be ready:

1. One must be saved by accepting Jesus Christ as Lord and Savior.

2. One must strive to live a righteous lifestyle. One must quickly confess and repent when they sin.

3. One must be performing the works of service God has called them to performed.

Regardless of what time period saints live in, they must, by the power of the Holy Ghost, remain faithful to Jesus Christ. Before the Tribulation Period begins, while the Tribulation Period is occurring, and after the Tribulation ends; saints must remain faithful to Jesus Christ. Daily pray asking God to always, and at all times, keep you faithful to Christ.

1. Study the scriptures for yourself while asking God the Father, in Jesus' name, to reveal to you, which view of when the Rapture occurs, does He desires you to hold to.

2. **Regardless of the view of the Rapture you hold; it will not change the sequence of end time events.**

3. As you read and study the Holy Bible; this book, and other books concerning end time events; pray asking God to show you how many of the events happening in our world today are fulfillment of end time prophecies.

Doing the things listed above will make you rapture ready.

The Tribulation Period

The Tribulation Period. This time period will begin at the time when the antichrist makes a seven-year peace treaty between Israel and her enemies. The Tribulation Period will last 7 years and will include all of the events in the Book of Revelation from chapter 6 through chapter 20:1-2. The second 3 ½ years of this seven-year period will be called "The Great Tribulation Period." (Matthew 24:21). We will discuss the Tribulation Period in greater details at the latter end of this book, however, we will now mention a few events which will happen during that time.

A. The antichrist will make a seven-year peace treaty between Israel and her enemies. However; He will break that peace treaty after 3 ½ years.

B. The seven seals (including the four horsemen).

C. The sealing of the 144,000 Jewish servants of God.

D. A time of great and untold national disasters (great earthquakes, hailstones mixed with fire, the sun, moon, and stars not shining, the moon turning to blood, etc.).

E. The seven trumpets (demonic spirits coming to torment and/or kill men).

F. The three woes.

G. The two witnesses.

H. satan kicked out of heaven.

I. The beast out of the sea.

J. The beast out of the earth.

K. The mark of the beast 666.

L. The seven angels of Revelation chapter 14.

M. MYSTERY Babylon.

N. The destruction of Babylon.

O. The coming of Jesus Christ with His church to fight the battle of Armageddon. The antichrist and the false prophet will be cast into the Lake of Fire.

P. The devil bound in the bottomless pit for 1000 years.

Q. And much, much, more as revealed in the book of Revelation, and in other prophetic books of the Holy Bible.

While many, many more events will transpire during this time period, we wanted you to be familiar with the term "The Tribulation Period.

Jesus is LORD

Father; thank You for including me, and all saints, for salvation in Your eternal plans and purposes. I am so blessed to be a child of Yours. In Jesus' name I pray; amen.

Jesus my LORD; thank You for securing salvation for all who would receive it by receiving You as Lord and Savior. Thank You for saving my soul. I love You, thank You, and forever worship You. I cherish spending eternity with You and with the Father.

Father; You may change in the way You deal with mankind; however, Your character and personality will never change. Regardless of what time period, or dispensation, we live in, You will remain, holy, loving, merciful, kind, caring, all-powerful, all-mighty, and all-knowing. Your grace, mercy, love, and blessings will come to all who call on You through Christ. Thank You my Father; In Jesus' name I pray; amen.

Jesus my LORD; thank You for making available the grace of God during all time periods.

Major Events That Will Happen In The Last Days

Always remember
Psalms 91

Regardless of what may happen in this world, and when it may happen; the promises of God found in Psalm 91 will always cover His children.

1. He that dwelleth in the secret place of the most High shall abide under the shadow of the Almighty.

2. I will say of the LORD, *He is* my refuge and my fortress: my God; in him will I trust.

3. Surely he shall deliver thee from the snare of the fowler, *and* from the noisome pestilence.

4. He shall cover thee with his feathers, and under his wings shalt thou trust: his truth *shall be thy* shield and buckler.

5. Thou shalt not be afraid for the terror by night; *nor* for the arrow *that* flieth by day;

6. *Nor* for the pestilence *that* walketh in darkness; *nor* for the destruction *that* wasteth at noonday.

7. A thousand shall fall at thy side, and ten thousand at thy right hand; *but* it shall not come nigh thee.

8. Only with thine eyes shalt thou behold and see the reward of the wicked.

9. Because thou hast made the LORD, *which is* my refuge, *even* the most High, thy habitation;

10. There shall no evil befall thee, neither shall any plague come nigh thy dwelling.

11. For he shall give his angels charge over thee, to keep thee in all thy ways.

12. They shall bear thee up in *their* hands, lest thou dash thy foot against a stone.

13. Thou shalt tread upon the lion and adder: the young lion and the dragon shalt thou trample under feet.

14. Because he hath set his love upon me, therefore will I deliver him: I will set him on high, because he hath known my name.

15. He shall call upon me, and I will answer him: I *will be* with him in trouble; I will deliver him, and honour him.

16. With long life will I satisfy him, and show him my salvation.

Learning to live under God's protection while flowing in the fullness of His Power.

In the midst of end time events unfolding in our world today, saints must learn to live under the protection of God, and flow in the Power of God. We must learn to live in victory over the world, the flesh, and the devil. Through daily meditating on the Word, seeking God in prayer, and worshiping God in spirit and in truth; we live in constant victory.

Saints must confess the Word at all times, plead the blood of the Lamb over our circumstances, and use the word of our testimony in every situation. Victory was won for us by Jesus Christ at the Cross; therefore, saints must increase in living in our Christ given victory.

> *(1ˢᵗ John.5:4-5) ⁴For whatsoever is born of God overcometh the world: and this is the victory that overcometh the world, even our faith. ⁵Who is he that overcometh the world, but he that believeth that Jesus is the Son of God?*
>
> *(2ⁿᵈ Corinthians.2:14) ¹⁴Now thanks be unto God, which always causeth us to triumph in Christ, and maketh manifest the savour of his knowledge by us in every place.*

Major events that will happen in the last days

(Matthew. 24:33-34) *³³So likewise ye, when ye shall see all these things, know that it is near, even at the doors. ³⁴Verily I say unto you, This generation shall not pass, till all these things be fulfilled.*

(Luke. 21:28) *²⁸And when these things begin to come to pass, then look up, and lift up your heads; for your redemption draweth nigh.*

> We will briefly mention these things and further expound upon them in a different section of this book.

As I update this book and notice (1) the pandemic that's occurring worldwide, (2) the uproar in race relationships, (3) judicial and law enforcement injustice, (4) political corruption, (5) adverse environmental conditions (earthquakes, floods, hurricanes, forest fires, droughts, etc.) (6) increase in gun violence (and all violence), and (7) so much, much more; I realize that end time events are happening in our midst, and is escalating in intensity and duration. In this section of our book we will briefly mention some of the major events prophesied to occur during the end times. However, we will expound on them in greater details later in this book.

Father; Thank You for blessing me to write this book. Please anoint me to teach; and please anoint readers to receive it, understand it, and live their lives according to the things You reveal to them. In Jesus name I pray; amen.

1. God will pour out His Spirit on all flesh to empower them to witness, prophesy, receive dreams, and receive visions.

(Acts.2:17-18) [17] And it shall come to pass in the last days, saith God, I will pour out of my Spirit upon all flesh: and your sons and your daughters shall prophesy, and your young men shall see visions, and your old men shall dream dreams: [18] And on my servants and on my handmaidens I will pour out in those days of my Spirit; and they shall prophesy:

(Acts.1:8) [8] But ye shall receive power, after that the Holy Ghost is come upon you: and ye shall be witnesses unto me both in Jerusalem, and in all Judaea, and in Samaria, and unto the uttermost part of the earth.

A. God pouring out His Spirit on saints to indwell them started on the Day of Pentecost (Acts.2:1-4). This is when the church began; and is also when the Dispensation of Grace began.

B. As we draw closer and closer to the coming of Jesus Christ, more and more saints of God will be filled with the Holy Ghost.

C. As we draw closer and closer to the coming of Jesus Christ, God will speak to more people through dreams and visions. He will speak to saints and sinners through dreams and visions.

> God knew that in the last days, saints would need dreams and visions in order to live in victory over the enemy. Because they are available to saints; ask God to give you dreams and visions of things to come.

D. Sinners will **dream dreams** revealing to them that Jesus Christ is the only way of salvation.

E. Sinners will **see visions** revealing to them that Jesus Christ is the only way of Salvation. The greatest increase in sinners having these dreams and visions will be in countries where the Gospel of Jesus Christ is outlawed.

F. Saints will receive dreams and visions warning them of things to come, and giving them instructions on things God wants them to do.

G. Pray asking God to constantly pour out His Spirit on You so you can have dreams and visions if it so be His will.

Because of His great love for sinners and saints, God pours His Spirit on both. God wants sinners saved; and saints matured in the things of Him. It is only by the Spirit of God that sinners can realize they need to be saved, and saints can live in the fullness of all God has for them.

Father; thank You for pouring out Your Spirit on all flesh. Thank You for working in both sinners and saints to reveal Your love, grace, and power. In Jesus' name I pray; amen.

Father; thank You for empowering Your saints for end time events. You placed Your Holy Spirit in us to give us victory, authority, and power over the world the flesh, and the devil. Please keep saints filled with Your Spirit; in Jesus' name I pray; amen.

Jesus my LORD; thank You for making the Holy Spirit available to all flesh; especially to the household of faith. When I think of the suffering You had to endure to bring us salvation, the Holy Spirit, and all the blessings of salvation; I worship You, love You, and live for You. I trust You, obey You, and serve You. You are truly an awesome, amazing, and outstanding Savior who is worthy of our greatest praise.

2. Israel will become an independent nation again. It's called in scripture "the fig tree"

(Matthew.24:32) ³²Now learn a parable of the fig tree; When his branch is yet tender, and putteth forth leaves, ye know that summer is nigh:

A. Israel became a nation again in 1948. This was prophecy being fulfilled.

B. End time prophecies could not totally be fulfilled until Israel became an independent nation again, because most end time events centers around Israel.

C. Israel also had to gain control of Jerusalem. That happened in 1967 during what is called "the Six Day War".

> **While God will deal with all nations; He will use Israel as His prophetic time clock to reveal to saints when and how these events will unfold. Keep your eyes on Israel.**

Although Israel had ceased from being a nation for hundreds of years, in the last days just before the return of Jesus Christ, Biblical prophecy says Israel will become a nation again. In 1948 Israel once again became an independent nation. As Israel began to bud like a young fig tree and put forth leaves of being a mighty and prosperous nation with a powerful military (that most likely possess nuclear weapons), it alerted all prophecy buffs that we are truly near the Rapture of the church (i.e. if the Rapture happens before the Tribulation Period begins), and we are living in the last of the last days.

While God will deal with the entire world, and His judgment and wrath will be poured out on sinful men of all races, kingdoms, and nations, **the focal point will be the Jews, the nation of Israel, and how all nations and people relate to her**. That is why the majority of the prophecies from the book of Daniel, Revelation, and other Biblical prophetic books concerning the last days, centers on the Jews, the nation of Israel, and on how other nations, people, and the antichrist relate to her.

God's chosen people of the Old Testament were the Jews; however, God's chosen people of the New Testament are those who have accepted Jesus Christ as Lord and Savior; regardless of race, creed, or color. Because of the faith and obedience of Abraham, God chose his descendants to be His chosen people. Because of the faith, obedience, and redemptive work of Jesus Christ, God chose all who receives Jesus as His chosen people.

As you advance in studying this book You will learn how and why God uses Israel as a prophetic time clock. Parents; God chose the Jew, blessed the Jews, and made an eternal covenant with the Jews because of Abraham. If you trust God, obey God, and love God as Abraham did, God will bless your descendants, use your descendants, and prosper your descendants for your sake.

Father; thank You for choosing as Your chosen people today, all who accept Jesus Christ as their Lord and Savior. Thank You for being a God who blesses the descendants of those who love You and keep Your commandments. In Jesus' name I pray; amen.

Jesus my LORD; while many end time prophetic events centers around the Jews, end time prophecy is all about You, Your love, and Your eternal plan and purpose. Thank You for including me, and all saints in your eternal plan for the ages.

3. Natural disasters will increase in frequency and intensity (the earth will be in travail)

(Romans.8:22) ²²For we know that the whole creation groaneth and travaileth in pain together until now.

(1st Thessalonians.5:3) ³For when they shall say, Peace and safety; then sudden destruction cometh upon them, as travail upon a woman with child; and they shall not escape.

A. The earth will be in travail (see the section of our book entitled the physical creation #1).

B. (Earth's environment and weather conditions will become worse and worse until it reaches the worst it has ever been since the creation of the world).

C. Earthquakes, tornados, volcanic eruptions, hurricanes, violent storms, droughts, extremely hot and extremely cold temperatures, record breaking snow storms, forest fires, mud-slides, etc., will increase and intensify.

D. Travailing things will happen, calm down for a while, and eventually worse travailing things will happen. Travailing times will constantly increase in frequency and intensity.

E. Although these things will happen and become worse and worse; many will not realize these things are signs of the times being fulfilled.

As the coming of Jesus Christ draws nearer and nearer, earth's environment will become more and more unstable. Things will be bad one year, then calm down for a few years, and then worse things will transpire. Records will be broken, unexplainable things will happen, and no one will be able to stop these things. If you have notice world-wide environmental conditions over the past few years, you should be able to tell that strange things are happening, and our environment is becoming worse and worse with the passing of time.

Saints of God, when travailing conditions happen in your area, God will either allow you to stop the travailing conditions in your area (Mark.4:35-41), or He will cause you to prevail over them (Acts.27:21-25) (Matthew.14:22-26). When God does not stop the travailing conditions for you, He will protect you and deliver you.

In travailing times, and during natural disasters; pray, trust God, and quote the promises of protection found in the written Word of God. God will keep His promises to you, protect you, and provide for you. Worship Him, trust Him, and obey Him.

Father; in all times, and in all conditions I will call on You. Thank You for being an ever present God, especially in times of trouble, travail, and tribulations. In Jesus' name I pray; amen.

Jesus my LORD; thank You for revealing to saints things to come. Thank You for empowering us by the Holy Ghost to endure all we encounter. Thank You for being with us, comforting us, and delivering us. I love You my Lord, Savior, and Redeemer.

4. False Christs and false prophets will increase more and more

(Matthew.24:5,11,24) [5]For many shall come in my name, saying, I am Christ; and shall deceive many. [11]And many false prophets shall rise, and shall deceive many [24]For there shall arise false Christs, and false prophets, and shall show great signs and wonders; insomuch that, if it were possible, they shall deceive the very elect.

(Mark.13:22-23) [22]For false Christs and false prophets shall rise, and shall show signs and wonders, to seduce, if it were possible, even the elect. [23]But take ye heed: behold, I have foretold you all things.

Great deception is on the way. Yea; great deception is already here. Beware; because God has foretold you. The greatest deception will be religious deception.

A. False prophets, false teachers, and false Christs with false religions will come deceiving many.

B. As we draw closer and closer to the coming of the real Christ many false Christs will begin to surface. Many will even teach from the Holy Bible but will misinterpret it in such ways that many people will be deceived and drawn away from Jesus Christ.

C. These false Christ will have the ability to work miracles, lying signs, and deceiving wonders. Because of their miracles, many will be drawn to them.

D. We are living in a time where saints must know the Holy Bible for themselves, and be determined to stick with its true teachings.

The major goal of the devil is to deceive people into going to hell with him. To accomplish that goal, he will use whatever he can. The devil will even use religion through false prophets, false teachers, and false preachers.

These false prophets, teachers,
and preachers will:

A. Work to keep people from accepting Jesus Christ as their Lord and Savior.

B. Cause saints to become involved in sin.

C. Bring false doctrine into many churches.

D. Cause many servants of God to abandon their service.

E. Work to make many true saints lukewarm.

F. Destroy Christian marriages; and Christian families.

G. Keep saints from living for God, loving God, trusting God, and worshiping God.

H. Much, much more.

Father; please continue working in saints to reveal to them who these false prophets, teachers, and preachers are; and how to avoid them. In Jesus' name I pray; amen.

Jesus my LORD; I trust You to keep me from being a false prophet, teacher, and preacher.

5. Iniquity shall increase and abound more and more

(Matthew.24:12) ¹²And because iniquity shall abound, the love of many shall wax cold.

A. Stealing, killing, rape, lying, and all types of iniquity will abound and increase in the last days. Man's inhumanity to man will begin to escalate just before and during the Tribulation Period.

B. Even big corporations and governments will become steeped in crime and illegal activity. They will rob the poor and take advantage of the needy. Many politicians will become corrupt and will constantly be involved in shady activities. Politicians will promise one thing but will do another after they are elected.

> **While sinners will decrease in love; disciples of Christ will be known because of their love. (John.13:35) 35 By this shall all men know that ye are my disciples, if ye have love one to another.**

C. Many nations and political leaders will take sinful wicked things which was once considered immoral and/or illegal, and make them legal and acceptable practices in society.

One of the worse things about iniquity abounding is that iniquity will fill the church. Many church leaders will live sinful and wicked lifestyles. Many saints will worship God Sunday morning, but will live sinful lifestyle Sunday evening and all week long. They will love the world, and the things of this world. Many will be corrupted by flattery, intoxicants, and pleasures of this world.

Regardless of how good God is to mankind, and regardless of how technologically advance they become, they will continue in their sins, iniquities and acts of unrighteousness. Man's inhumanity to man will escalate as we draw closer and closer to the coming of Christ. It is sad to think that instead of things becoming better; they are becoming worse.

> *(2nd Timothy.3:1-3) ¹This know also, that in the last days perilous times shall come. ²For men shall be lovers of their own selves, covetous, boasters, proud, blasphemers, disobedient to parents, unthankful, unholy, ³Without natural affection, trucebreakers, false accusers, incontinent, fierce, despisers of those that are good, ⁴Traitors, heady, highminded, lovers of pleasures more than lovers of God; ⁵Having a form of godliness, but denying the power thereof: from such turn away. ⁶For of this sort are they which creep into houses, and lead captive silly women laden with sins, led away with divers lusts.*

Father; in the midst of iniquity abounding and perilous times; please help Your saints to live holy, righteous, and godly lifestyles. In Jesus' name I pray; amen.

Jesus my LORD; You died to make me holy. You sent the Holy Ghost to help me make my life holy. You want holy saints living holy lifestyles.

6. The love of many will wax cold

(Matthew.24:12) *¹²And because iniquity shall abound, the love of many shall wax cold.*

In the last days just before the coming of Jesus Christ the enemy of our souls will work hard to make people loveless people filled with hate, envy, and evil. The enemy will work:

A. To take love out of homes.

B. To keep spouses (even Christian spouses) from loving one another as God desires them to.

C. To keep children from loving parents, and parents from loving children.

D. To take love out of society, and out of the world.

As we draw closer and closer to the coming of Jesus Christ you will begin to notice that love will decrease while hate will increase. People will become cold hearted people devoid of love, kindness, and compassion. They will misuse and mistreat one another without feelings of guilt, shame or regret. Even saints will lose their first love. They will not love Jesus Christ with all their hearts. Jesus will say to them;

> *(Revelation.2:4)* *⁴Nevertheless I have somewhat against thee,* **_because thou hast left thy first love_**.

In the sight of God, love is the most important thing. We are to love God with all our heart, soul, and mind; and we are to love others as we love our self (Matthew.22:37-38).

Regardless of what a person does, if they do it without love; they are nothing, and it prophets them nothing in the sight of God (1ˢᵗ Corinthians.13:1-3).

Saints are to be different. We are to be known by our love for God and for others.

> *(John.13:34-35).* *³⁴A new commandment I give unto you, That ye love one another; as I have loved you, that ye also love one another. ³⁵By this shall all men know that ye are my disciples, if ye have love one to another.*
>
> *(1ˢᵗ John.4:7-8) ⁷Beloved, let us love one another: for love is of God; and every one that loveth is born of God, and knoweth God. ⁸He that loveth not knoweth not God; for God is love.*

While sinners are decreasing in love; saints are to increase in love. Regardless of the cost, and regardless of the consequences; saints are to love to the fullest of their ability. Their love is to glorify God, lift up Jesus Christ, and demonstrate the power of the Holy Ghost.

Father; please anoint saints to love You to the fullest, and to love others as You desire us to. We must allow our love to shine to Your glory, honor, and praise. We must also glorify Jesus with our love. In Jesus' name I pray; amen.

Jesus my LORD; God is love (1ˢᵗ John.4:8); the Father so loved (John.3:16), and God commended His love (Romans.5:8). Because of the importance of love in Your sight, and in the sight of the Father; saints must major in being people of love; real love.

> *(1ˢᵗ John.3:17-18) ¹⁷But whoso hath this world's good, and seeth his brother have need, and shutteth up his bowels of compassion from him, how dwelleth the love of God in him? ¹⁸My little children, let us not love in word, neither in tongue; but in deed and in truth.*

7. Many saints will be strong and will do exploits

(Daniel.11:23) ³²And such as do wickedly against the covenant shall he corrupt by flatteries: but the people that do know their God shall be strong, and do exploits.

Saints must realize we are in spiritual battle against the forces of darkness (Ephesians.6:10-12). We must put on the whole armor of God (Ephesians.6:13-18), take up the weapons of our warfare (2nd Corinthians10:4-6), and become empowered by the gifts of the Spirit (1st Corinthians.12:1-11). As soldiers (2nd Timothy.2:3-4) in the army of the Lord; we must fight the good fight of faith (1st Timothy.6:12).

> **Instead of the devil being too strong for me to handle; I will be too strong for him to handle. I will be too strong for him because I daily grow in the knowledge of God.**

Saints must rise to levels where the enemy of our souls can not handle us, deal with us, nor stand against us. We must live in, walk in, and function in the victory Jesus Christ has won for us.

(1st John.4:4) Ye are of God, little children, and have overcome them: because greater is he that is in you, than he that is in the world.

(1st Corinthians.15:57-58) ⁵⁷But thanks be to God, which giveth us the victory through our Lord Jesus Christ. ⁵⁸Therefore, my beloved brethren, be ye stedfast, unmoveable, always abounding in the work of the Lord, forasmuch as ye know that your labour is not in vain in the Lord.

While a lot of bad and evil things will transpire in the last days, the true servants of the Savior will be strong and will do exploit.

As saints increase in the knowledge of who God is, the stronger they will become and the greater exploits they will do.

Saints who are weak in the faith and who are lacking in the knowledge of God will not be strong, will not do exploits, and will be corrupted by flatteries.

> *(Luke.9:1) ¹Then he called his twelve disciples together, and gave them power and authority over all devils, and to cure diseases. (Matthew.10:1) ¹And when he had called unto him his twelve disciples, he gave them power against unclean spirits, to cast them out, and to heal all manner of sickness and all manner of disease.*

Father; thank You for giving saints all they need to be strong in You, and to overcome all the attacks of the enemy. Because of the redemptive work of the Lord Jesus Christ, we are more than conquerors (Romans.8:37), and we always triumph (2nd Corinthians2:14). Thank You for victory. In Jesus' name I pray; amen.

Jesus my LORD; thank You for the victory of Your Cross.

8. Many saints will have a form of godliness but have no power manifesting in their lives.

(2nd Timothy.3:5) ⁵Having a form of godliness, but denying the power thereof: from such turn away.

A. Many saints will lack the power needed to live righteous lives, to overcome the attacks of the enemy, and to be lights in the midst of this darken world. They will see no miracles in their lives, and they will not be Spirit filled.

B. Because of a lack of knowledge, many saints will have a lack of faith; which will lead to a lack of power; which will lead to destruction. *(Hosea.4:6a) ⁶My people are destroyed for lack of knowledge:*

C. This lack of power and spiritual growth upsets the Lord Jesus Christ. *(Hebrews.5:12-13) ¹²For when for the time ye ought to be teachers, ye have need that one teach you again which be the first principles of the oracles of God; and are become such as have need of milk, and not of strong meat.*

Saints of God must rise up and begin walking in the fullness of the Power God has made available to saints through the redemptive work of Jesus Christ. We must learn to allow the Holy Spirit to so work in us that God is able to do exceeding, abundantly, and above all we ask or think.

(Ephesians.3:20) ²⁰Now unto him that is able to do exceeding abundantly above all that we ask or think, according to the power that worketh in us.

To increase in power

A. To increase in power, saints must increase in prayer.

B. To increase in power, saints must increase in the knowledge of the written Word of God.

C. To increase in power, saints must increase in worshiping God in spirit and in truth.

D. To increase in power, saints must increase in loving God.

E. To increase in power, saints must increase in faith.

F. To increase in power, saints must increase in staying away from powerless saints.

Saints must never become content with living on the same level spiritually. They must constantly elevate to higher and higher levels in Christ. They must constantly increase in power, praise, service, faith, righteous living, love, and walking in victory over the devil. As they increase in these things and more, they increase in power.

Father; because of increased demonic activity in this world, saints must increase in flowing in spiritual power. We must learn to abandon our weak physical power, and flow in Your power to Your glory. In Jesus' name I pray; amen. *(2nd Corinthians.4:7) ^{7}But we have this treasure in earthen vessels, that the excellency of the power may be of God, and not of us.*

Jesus my LORD; thank You for giving us Power; and thank You for teaching us to daily live in the fullness of the Power You have given us.

9. Evil men and seducers shall become worse and worse

(2ⁿᵈ Timothy.3:13) ¹³But evil men and seducers shall wax worse and worse, deceiving, and being deceived.

A. Each generation will become more sinful until iniquity fills the world.

B. Television programs will become filled with sex and violence. Music will be filled with foul language and wicked messages.

C. All of society will move further and further away from God and from the righteousness He demands in His written Word.

It would seem that as mankind increases in technology, they would increase in integrity. However, it seems that the more God blesses them with technological advancements, the more they increase in transgressions, terrible living, and treacherous behavior. While their physical lives are becoming better; their hearts are becoming worse and worse. Instead of giving their lives to God in praise, worship, and thanksgiving; they give their hearts to satan, sin, and sadistic living. Instead of using their advance technology to help others, they use it to destroy others. Regardless of how advanced society become, evil men and seducers will become worse and worse.

Saints must not allow evil men, seducers, and deceiving people to cause them to live in sin against their Savior. Saints must shine as bright lights to the glory of God the Father. We must overcome evil with good, overpower hate with love, and overthrow wickedness with righteousness. We must live holy, godly, and sanctified lifestyles which will show the world we belong to Jesus Christ.

(Philippians.2:15) ¹⁵That ye may be blameless and harmless, the sons of God, without rebuke, in the midst of a crooked and perverse nation, among whom ye shine as lights in the world;

Father; please help me to shine to Your glory, honor, and praise. Please help me to be as bright a light for Jesus Christ as He desires me to be. In Jesus' name I pray; amen.

> *(Matthew.5:16)* [16]*Let your light so shine before men, that they may see your good works, and glorify your Father which is in heaven.*

Jesus my Lord; I refuse to hide in the darkness of this world. I must overcome darkness with the light of Your love and Power, so You may be glorified in the sight of all mankind.

10. Children will become disobedient to parents

(2nd Timothy.3:2) ^{2}For men shall be lovers of their own selves, covetous, boasters, proud, blasphemers, disobedient to parents, unthankful, unholy,

A. With the passing of each generation children will become worse and worse.

B. Children will become increasingly disobedient to parents and those in authority.

C. Children will fall away from God and church.

D. Children will become involved in drugs, crime, gangs, sex, and many other sinful behaviors.

> **Why are so many parents mad that their children are living like the devil when they have not taught their children the ways of Christ? If you want them to live like Jesus, teach them about Jesus.**

E. Children will call good things and good people **bad**. They will call bad things and bad people **good**. Good kids are called nerds, geeks, and uncool kids; while bad kids are called cool.

F. Many children will turn to false religions or to no religion at all.

G. Many children will acknowledge God and Jesus Christ but will not live for Them.

It is important for parents to pray for their children, become good Christian examples for their children, and teach their children the Word of God. We must rebuke the devil, bind the devil, and cast out the devil so he will not influence our children in wicked and sinful ways. We must encourage our children to accept Jesus Christ as their Lord and Savior; and ask God to keep them filled with the Holy Ghost. We must do all we can, with what we can, and as often as we can, to empower our children to love Jesus, live for Jesus, and serve Jesus Christ all the days of their lives.

(Proverbs.22:6) 6. Train up a child in the way he should go: and when he is old, he will not depart from it.

Father; I have applied into my life the principles and teachings of scripture concerning children. Thank You for teaching me those things, and thank You for honoring those things in the lives of my children. My children are saved, sanctified, and filled with Your Holy Spirit. Please continue to cause them to advance in You. In Jesus' name I pray; amen.

(Psalms.127:3-4) 3 Lo, children are an heritage of the LORD: and the fruit of the womb is his reward. 4 As arrows are in the hand of a mighty man; so are children of the youth.

Jesus my LORD; thank You for the children You have blessed me with. Thank You for making me a good father to them. I rejoice in knowing all my children are saved, and are striving to live for You. I trust You to keep them all the days of their lives, and even forever more. I love You my Lord.

11. Sexual perversion, homosexuality, and immorality will increase and become worse and worse

(2nd Timothy.3:6) ⁶For of this sort are they which creep into houses, and lead captive silly women laden with sins, led away with divers lusts,

(Revelation.9:21) ²¹Neither repented they of their murders, nor of their sorceries, nor of their fornication, nor of their thefts.

(Romans.1:26-27) ²⁶For this cause God gave them up unto vile affections: for even their women did change the natural use into that which is against nature: ²⁷And likewise also the men, leaving the natural use of the woman, burned in their lust one toward another; men with men working that which is unseemly, and receiving in themselves that recompense of their error which was meet.

A. Sexual immorality will fill the world (fornication, adultery, homosexuality, pornography, pedophilia, etc.).

B. Television, the internet, the printed page, and other forms of entertainment will be filled with sex, immorality, and perversion. People will even dress in sexually enticing ways. The saddest part about all this is that many saints will become involved in immorality.

C. Saints are to always choose living sanctified in the Savior and avoid sinful sexual seductions.

All saints should daily and constantly pray asking God to lead them not into temptation, and to deliver them from evil. We must resolve in our hearts to live holy, righteous, and godly lifestyles. We must sanctify the Lord Jesus in our hearts in such ways that we do not sin against Him.

> *(1ˢᵗ Peter.3:15)* ¹⁵*But sanctify the Lord God in your hearts: and be ready always to give an answer to every man that asketh you a reason of the hope that is in you with meekness and fear:*

Father; when I think about how awesome You are, and how good You have been to me, I refuse to place sex and immorality before You. I purpose by the power of the Holy Ghost to live holy, righteous, and godly in these last days. I refuse to allow Jesus to come and catch me living in fornication, adultery, homosexuality, or any sexual impurities. I am kept by Your Power, and I trust You to keep me from falling. In Jesus' name I pray; amen.

> *(Jude.1:24-25)* ²⁴*Now unto him that is able to keep you from falling, and to present you faultless before the presence of his glory with exceeding joy,* ²⁵*To the only wise God our Saviour, be glory and majesty, dominion and power, both now and for ever. Amen.*

Jesus my LORD; thank You for being my righteousness and my sustainer. By Your Power I will live a sanctified lifestyle.

12. Many saints will receive more pleasure from the things of this world than from the things of God

(Romans.1:32) ³²Who knowing the judgment of God, that they which commit such things are worthy of death, not only do the same, but have pleasure in them that do them.

A. Many saints will become involved in the sinful activity that sinners become involved in.

B. Many saints will enjoy secular entertainment more than spiritual things. They will watch television programs that sinners watch, and will listen to the music sinners listen to.

> **What brings you your greatest form of entertainment; secular things or spiritual things?**

C. Many saints will become more excited about secular things than spiritual things. They will shout and rejoice over ball games while remaining silent and unemotional at church.

When I see what saints watch on television, and what they view on the internet, I am convinced that most enjoy the things of this world more than the things of God. God tells us to set our minds on things which are true, honest, just, pure, lovely, and of good report; however, we watch violence, immorality, contentions, and strife all day long on television. The more surprising thing about it all is that their conscience does not bother them, trouble them, nor reveal to them that what they are watching is displeasing to God. Did God really mean it when He said *(Philippians.4:8) ⁸Finally, brethren, whatsoever things are true, whatsoever things are honest, whatsoever things are just, whatsoever things are pure, whatsoever things are lovely, whatsoever things are of good report; if there be any virtue, and if there be any praise, think on these things.*

Does it really make a difference what we watch on television? Is God holding us accountable for what we watch on television? Does what we watch on television have any effect on our spirit and soul?

(Psalms.101:2-3) ² *I will behave myself wisely in a perfect way. O when wilt thou come unto me? I will walk within my house with a perfect heart.* ³ **<u>I will set no wicked thing before mine eyes:</u>** *I hate the work of them that turn aside; it shall not cleave to me.*

Father; I ask You to help me to only watch on television, the internet, and on the cell phone; only those things which are pleasing and acceptable in Your sight. Please reveal to me when I am watching something, or doing something displeasing to You. In Jesus' name I pray; amen.

Jesus my LORD; I want everything I do, say, and watch to be pleasing and acceptable to You. I want You to be Lord over what I watch on television.

13. Crime and violence will escalate

(Revelation.9:21) ²¹Neither repented they of their murders, nor of their sorceries, nor of their fornication, nor of their thefts.

A. If you were to notice crime statistics, you will realize that murder and crime is at an all-time high throughout the world.

B. From small time hoods, to corporate crimes, to political corruption, to police and judicial injustice, and much, much more; crime is on an increase; and it will get worse and worse.

C. Many people in the name of religion will commit horrible crimes against those of their own religion and those of other religions.

While dark days are on the way, saints have no need to fear. In the midst of escalating crime and violence; God will be with His children, will protect His children, and will deliver His children out of harm's way.

(Hebrews.13:5-6) Let your conversation be without covetousness; and be content with such things as ye have: for he hath said, I will never leave thee, nor forsake thee. ⁶So that we may boldly say, The Lord is my helper, and I will not fear what man shall do unto me.

Saints must start their day praying for God's protection for themselves, their loved ones, and for all people. We must walk in wisdom, follow the leading of the Holy Spirit, and, trust that God's angels are protecting us. We must not live in fear, and we must acknowledge God in all our ways so He can direct us away from the path of evil and wicked people. *(Proverbs.3:5-6) ⁵Trust in the LORD with all thine heart; and lean not unto thine own understanding. ⁶In all thy ways acknowledge him, and he shall direct thy paths.*

Even in the midst of increasing and escalating crime and violence; Psalms.91 will still be in effect for God's saints. When wicked and ungodly men try to come against saints, we can cry unto the Lord and He will deliver us out of their hands (Psalms.18:4-6,17).

God wants saints to know what's coming, and to prepare for it. We must stay in prayer, live righteous lifestyle, and serve God with all our might. Doing these things and more will cause us to overcome all that wicked men and sinful men endeavor to do.

Father; thank You for being my fence of protection and my city of refuge. You are my high tower, and my strong tower. Thank You for preserving us from all evil. In Jesus' name I pray; amen.

Jesus my LORD; I will trust in Your protection. I will look to You at all times; even in times of trouble. Thank You for being with me, and for never leaving me.

14. Devil and demon worship will increase more and more

(1ˢᵗ Corinthians.10:20) ²⁰But I say, that the things which the Gentiles sacrifice, they sacrifice to devils, and not to God: and I would not that ye should have fellowship with devils.

(Revelation.9:20) ²⁰And the rest of the men which were not killed by these plagues yet repented not of the works of their hands, that they should not worship devils, and idols of gold, and silver, and brass, and stone, and of wood: which neither can see, nor hear, nor walk:

A. The world will be filled with demon worship, sorcery, and idolatry. Many will become involved in different kinds of wicked Occult practices.

B. Some people will know they are worshiping the devil, while others will worship him and not know they are worshiping him. The devil will deceive them into ignorantly worshiping him.

C. Whenever you worship anything or anyone other than God through His Son Jesus Christ, you are worshiping the devil. You may not know you are worshipping him, but you are.

D. Whenever you place anything before God or higher than God in your life, you are worshiping the devil.

E. As we come closer and closer to the return of Jesus Christ, satan worship and occult activity will constantly increase.

To ensure you are not unknowingly worshiping the devil, demons, and unclean spirits; become saved, live for God, and worship God only. Never place anyone or anything equal to God, above God, nor in front of God in your life. Make God the center of Your life; and in everything acknowledge Him. Talk about God, rejoice in God, and glory in Him. Focus your attention on Jesus Christ, and allow Him to be the source of Your joy and entertainment. Allow Jesus Christ to be Your everything.

Father; I want to be so busy worshiping You and Jesus Christ that I don't have time nor desire to worship anything or anyone else. Your praise shall continually be in my mouth. My soul shall make her boast of You. The humble shall hear and be glad. In Jesus' name I pray; amen.

> *(Psalms.34:1-3)* [1] *I will bless the LORD at all times: his praise shall continually be in my mouth.* [2] *My soul shall make her boast in the LORD: the humble shall hear thereof, and be glad.* [3] *O magnify the LORD with me, and let us exalt his name together.*

Jesus my LORD; You paid an extremely high price to place me in a position where I can worship You and the Father. I refuse to take the price of redemption for granted. I love You my Lord; and I will worship You all day long.

> *(Psalms.35:28)* [28] *And my tongue shall speak of thy righteousness and of thy praise all the day long.*

15. There will be a great falling away from the church and from the ways of God

(2nd Thessalonians.2:) ³Let no man deceive you by any means: for that day shall not come, except there come a falling away first, and that man of sin be revealed, the son of perdition;

A. Church attendance will decrease, and people will become less and less concerned about church, God, and the things of God.

B. Many of our religious freedoms will be taken away, and persecution of saints will begin to increase more and more.

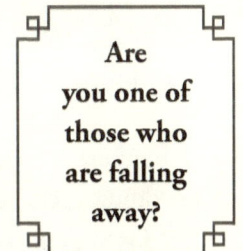

As awesome as God is, I don't understand how anyone can fall away from Him. As wonderful as His written Word is, I don't understand how anyone can abandon it. As much as Jesus Christ has done for us, I don't understand how anyone can turn away from Him. Yet; as we draw closer and closer to the return of Christ; there will be a great falling away.

Reasons people fall away
(Mark.4:14-20) and other scriptures

A. The devil stealing the Word from people before it has a chance to take root in their hearts.

B. Affliction and persecution coming upon them.

C. Many are caught up into the cares of this world. They are more concerned about physical things than spiritual things.

D. Many are chasing after the deceitfulness of riches. Because they are so busy working and making a living, they abandon the things of God.

E. The lust of other things.

F. People looking for religious doctrine they want instead of receiving the true doctrine of the Word.

G. People becoming entangled in wicked and sinful behavior.

H. People being drawn into false religion.

I. People having God in their heads, but not in their heart. They know a lot about Him in their heads, but they have no true love for Him in their hearts.

Knowing there will be a great falling away should cause you to greatly guard against doing such. Instead of decreasing in the things of God, and in your love for God; you should constantly increase in the things of God, and in your love for God. Daily intercede for others asking God to work to keep them from falling away.

Father; when I think of who You are, and all You have done, I refuse to allow the enemy of my soul to cause me to slack up on You, back up on You, or give up on You. I daily pray You will cause me to constantly increase in loving You. In Jesus' name I pray; amen.

Jesus my LORD; thank You for placing me in the Father's hands. He is well able to keep me from falling away. (John.10:28-29).

16. The gospel of the kingdom will be preached around the world

(Matthew.24:14) ¹⁴And this gospel of the kingdom shall be preached in all the world for a witness unto all nations; and then shall the end come.

A. While many negative things will happen, God will make sure that the gospel of Jesus Christ will be preached in all the world.

B. Through television, radio, internet, the printed page, and evangelistic crusades, this gospel will reach the entire world.

C. Sinners will have dreams and visions of people preaching the gospel to them, and will accept Jesus Christ once they awaken from their dreams and visions.

The time is short (1ˢᵗ Corinthians.7:29), the days are evil, and saints must redeem the time (Ephesians.5:16). All saints must be actively involved in spreading the gospel of Jesus Christ around the world. We must begin in our homes, on our jobs, in the market place, and everywhere we go. We need to support our churches, and support ministries who are working to spread the gospel around the world.

All saints need to be faithful in their duties and ministry. Prayer warriors need to return to prayer, teachers to teaching, preachers to preaching, and finance officers to dealing with the finances of the church. All servants of the Savior need to increase in service.

*(Luke.9:23) ²³And he said to them all, If any man will come after me, let him deny himself, and take up his cross **daily**, and follow me.*

Everyday, saints need to be involved in spreading the gospel of Jesus Christ. One of the greatest things saints can do is pray for souls to be saved. We also must be lights for Christ in this darkened world. Never be afraid to witness, and always be ready to give a testimony about the goodness of God.

(1ˢᵗ Peter.3:15) *¹⁵But sanctify the Lord God in your hearts: and be ready always to give an answer to every man that asketh you a reason of the hope that is in you with meekness and fear:*

Father; please empower and anoint saints to make full proof of their ministries. Thank You for providing to ministries, to ministers, and to saints everything needed to spread the gospel of Jesus Christ around the world. In Jesus' name I pray; amen.

Jesus my LORD; I trust in the Holy Ghost to use me as He pleases to spread Your gospel around the world. While I can not do everything, I can do my part. I daily and constantly want to do my part.

17. There will be wars and rumors of wars. Wars and military conflicts will escalate

(Matthew.24:6-7) *⁶And ye shall hear of wars and rumours of wars: <u>**see that ye be not troubled**</u>: for all these things must come to pass, but the end is not yet. ⁷For nation shall rise against nation, and kingdom against kingdom: and there shall be famines, and pestilences, and earthquakes, in divers places.*

> **Attendance at prayer meetings will decrease while wars will increase. Less prayer always leads to increased wars and conflicts.**

(Mark.13:7-8) *⁷And when ye shall hear of wars and rumours of wars, be ye not troubled: for such things must needs be; but the end shall not be yet. ⁸For nation shall rise against nation, and kingdom against kingdom: and there shall be earthquakes in divers places, and there shall be famines and troubles: these are the beginnings of sorrows.*

(Luke.21:9-10) *⁹But when ye shall hear of wars and commotions, be not terrified: for these things must first come to pass; but the end is not by and by. ¹⁰Then said he unto them, Nation shall rise against nation, and kingdom against kingdom:*

A. There will be wars and rumors of wars until the entire world is filled with wars (this will escalate during the Tribulation Period).

B. Times of conflicts, contentions, and wars are about to erupt upon this planet nationally and internationally.

C. Conflicts between nations and within nations will begin to erupt everywhere.

D. Tremendous advancements in military weapons, military technology, and military equipment will constantly increase and improve. Many nations will acquire weapons of mass destruction, and nuclear war will be a constant threat.

While we are briefly mentioning these things now, we will expound on them in greater details later in this book.

Knowing wars are about to erupt worldwide in the future should cause you to greatly enjoy and appreciate the peace times you now have. It should cause you to constantly pray that peace will prevail until the times of the end. When wars begin to occur, realize that God is still your God even in the midst of wars. Pray, trust Him, and do as He instructs you to do.

Father; You tell us of the impending wars to come; and then challenge us to be not troubled (Matthew.24:6). Saints must allow You to elevate our faith to such levels that not even wars can trouble or disturb us. Thank You for being our comfort in times of wars.

Jesus my LORD; trusting You is not just something saints talk about; it is something saints need to be about. In peace times we must daily strive to increase our faith in You. We must learn to develop unshakeable faith that will stand strong in you; even in times of war.

18. Sickness and disease will increase more and more

(Matthew.24:7) ⁷For nation shall rise against nation, and kingdom against kingdom: and there shall be famines, and pestilences, and earthquakes, in divers places (Luke.21:11) ¹¹And great earthquakes shall be in divers places, and famines, and pestilences; and fearful sights and great signs shall there be from heaven.

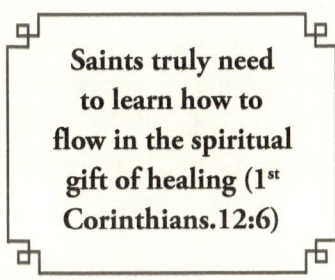

Saints truly need to learn how to flow in the spiritual gift of healing (1ˢᵗ Corinthians.12:6)

A. The world will be filled with **pestilences** (massive sicknesses that kills large numbers of people).

B. Sickness is going to constantly increase throughout the world and medical science will be unable to stop it (this will escalate during the Tribulation Period).

C. In the last days, contaminants from food, clothing, products, manufactured goods, and medicines will make people sick.

D. Even with great advancements in medical technology and drugs, sickness will abound and increase.

In times of sickness; saints are to use doctors, medicine, and medical technology; however, we are to trust God. It is God who makes medicine work as it supposed to. It is God who can heal even when medicine can't help us, or when medicine is not available.

(Exodus.15:26) ²⁶And said, If thou wilt diligently hearken to the voice of the LORD thy God, and wilt do that which is right in his sight, and wilt give ear to his commandments, and keep all his statutes, I will put none of these diseases upon thee,

which I have brought upon the Egyptians: for I am the LORD that healeth thee.

I will not dictate how God is to heal; I will just trust Him to do it. With or without medicine, I trust God to bring manifestation of healing to me. During times of sickness, I will pray, quote the Word, seek medical attention, worship God, call the pastor to anoint me with oil, and get saints of like precious faith to pray for me. I will do all God tells me to do in His written Word while trusting Him for healing.

(2nd Chronicles.15:12-13) ^{12}And Asa in the thirty and ninth year of his reign was diseased in his feet, until his disease was exceeding great: yet in his disease he sought not to the LORD, but to the physicians. ^{13}And Asa slept with his fathers, and died in the one and fortieth year of his reign.

Father; please help saints to trust You more than in physicians and medicine. You are the God who heal, thus I look to You for healing; even in the time of increased sicknesses I look to You. In Jesus' name I pray; amen.

Jesus my LORD; saints must advance to levels where we can see manifestation of healing in Your name. The greatest line of defense against sickness should be saints.

*(Mark.16:18) ^{18}They shall take up serpents; and if they drink any deadly thing, it shall not hurt them**; they shall lay hands on the sick, and they shall recover**.*

19. Many saints will flow in the Power of God

(Mark.16:17-18) ¹⁷And these signs shall follow them that believe; In my name shall they cast out devils; they shall speak with new tongues; ¹⁸They shall take up serpents; and if they drink any deadly thing, it shall not hurt them; they shall lay hands on the sick, and they shall recover.

> I must flow in all the Power God has made available to saints. Are you striving to flow in the fullness of God's Power?

Awesome, great, amazing, outstanding, and astonishing things should constantly be produced by the servants of Jesus Christ. Because of the redemptive work of Jesus Christ, and because we have the Greater one living in us, we should produce greater things than the world produces. In the last days, a remnant of saints will know God so well they will do exploits to the glory of God (Daniel.11:32).

(1ˢᵗ Corinthians.4:20) ²⁰For the kingdom of God is not in word, but in power.

God has empowered saints to

A. Love God with all their hearts, and love others as they love themselves.

B. Live holy, righteous, and godly lifestyles.

C. Rebuke, bind, and cast out devils.

D. See miracles manifest constantly in their lives and in the lives of others.

E. Heal the sick.

F. Overcome all the works of the enemy.

G. Overcome evil with good.

H. Move mountains.

I. Change circumstances, situations, and things according to the will of God.

J. To prosper abundantly spiritually, physically, and emotionally.

K. To live in joy, peace, and contentment.

L. So much, much more.

M. Saints have been empowered to do everything God wants them to do in their physical lives.

Daily pray asking God to fill you with the Holy Spirit and cause you to daily flow in the fullness of the power He has made available to saints.

Father; I want my life to naturally be supernatural to Your glory each and everyday. Because of all You have made available to saints through Jesus Christ; saints should be known as people of love, power, and righteousness. In Jesus' name I pray; amen.

Jesus my LORD; as I constantly increase in living in the Power You have made available to saints, I want the glory to go to You.

20. There will be massive shortages of food and of the necessary staples of life

*(Matthew.24:7) ⁷For nation shall rise against nation, and kingdom against kingdom: and there shall be **famines**, and pestilences, and earthquakes, in divers places (Mark.13:8) ⁸For nation shall rise against nation, and kingdom against kingdom: and there shall be earthquakes in divers places, and there shall be **famines** and troubles: these are the beginnings of sorrows. (Luke.21:11) ¹¹And great earthquakes shall be in divers places, and **famines**, and pestilences; and fearful sights and great signs shall there be from heaven*

A. Famines (massive shortages of food, clothing, medicine, and the necessities of life) will occur worldwide (this will escalate during the Tribulation Period).

B. Many of these shortages will be man-made (so they can control people) while others will be a result of worsening national disasters.

C. Saints of God will have to depend more and more on God supplying their needs. Saints must use wisdom, faith, and prayer; while looking to God for miracles of provisions and supplies.

Regardless of the negative conditions of the world, God will provide for His saints. *(Psalms.37:25) ²⁵ I have been young, and now am old; yet have I not seen the righteous forsaken, nor his seed begging bread.*

Even if He has to work miracles as He did for the children of Israel in the wilderness; God will provide for His children, and He will do it as long as He has to.

*(Psalms.33:18-20) ¹⁸ Behold, the eye of the LORD is upon them that fear him, upon them that hope in his mercy; ¹⁹ **To deliver their soul from death, and to keep them alive in famine.** ²⁰ Our soul waiteth for the LORD: he is our help and our shield.*

> *21 For our heart shall rejoice in him, because we have trusted in his holy name.*

Saints must always remember the promises of God, the Power of God, and the presence of God. God does through us the things we can do, and He does for us things we can't do. In everything, and for everything, we must look to God, trust in God, and depend on God. He will come through for You.

Father; thank You for being a God who keeps His promises. Regardless of situations, circumstances, or conditions, You will keep Your promises. Thank You for being a God in whom we can trust. In Jesus' name; amen.

Jesus my LORD; because God gave us You, who is the greatest of all things, how much more will He faithfully give us these lesser things. He gives us all things which pertain to life and godliness.

> *(Romans.8:32) ³²He that spared not his own Son, but delivered him up for us all, how shall he not with him also freely give us all things?*

21. Travel will increase; men will run to and fro

(Daniel.12:4) ⁴But thou, O Daniel, shut up the words, and seal the book, even to the time of the end: many shall run to and fro, and knowledge shall be increased.

A. As the coming of Jesus Christ draws near, men will be constantly traveling all over the world, and even into outer space.

B. Man-made modes of transportation will increase and improve. They will enable more people to reach different points in the world in shorter and shorter time periods. Local travel will increase in cities, counties, and states. Men will travel to and fro, locally, nationally and internationally.

As I look at modern technology I can easily see how they fit into last day prophecies. When the last day prophecies were spoken by the prophets, it seemed inconceivable for them to manifest. However, because of modern day technology; what was once inconceivable is now easily conceivable.

A. The advancement in military weaponry makes it conceivable that all life on earth can be killed (Matthew.24:22, Mark.13:20).

B. With the advancements in internet technology it is conceivable to see how no one can buy our sale without the mark of the beast. This represents a cashless society (Revelation.13:16-17).

C. With the invention and advancement of air travel; it is conceivable to see how many will run to and fro all over the earth. (Daniel.12:4)

As we look at air traffic, railway traffic, highway expansion, ships, submarines, bus traffic, and many, many more modern modes of transportation, we see Daniel's prophecy of many running to and fro being fulfilled.

End time prophecies are constantly being fulfilled in our midst. All saints need to pray asking God to show them how biblical prophecies are manifesting in our world today, and what we should be doing in light of them.

Father; as I see biblical prophecies manifesting before me, I realize Your Word is true, and You are the true and living God. Please reveal to me what You would have me do in light of these prophecies being fulfilled daily. In Jesus' name I pray; amen.

Jesus my LORD; I must allow the Holy Spirit to advance me to higher levels of service, and higher levels of glorifying Your name to the world. I do not want You to come and catch me with my work undone. Everyday I must be about my Father's business.

> *(Luke.2:49-50)* [49]*And he said unto them, How is it that ye sought me? wist ye not that I must be about my Father's business? Lord; I must be about my Father's business daily.*

22. Knowledge will increase and escalate

(Daniel. 12:4) ⁴But thou, O Daniel, shut up the words, and seal the book, even to the time of the end: many shall run to and fro, and knowledge shall be increased.

A. Knowledge will increase dramatically as we draw closer and closer to the coming of Jesus Christ.

B. Sinful men will accomplish such high levels of intellectual secular knowledge that it will draw them further and further away from God.

C. Sinful men will depend so much on knowledge, science, and technology that they will feel they don't need God.

> **Sinners will constantly increase in secular knowledge while saints will decrease in the true knowledge of God. Are you decreasing or increasing in the knowledge of God?**

The physically wiser men become, the less they depend on God. As they increase in scientific knowledge they will decrease in spiritual dependency upon the Savior. They will call on God less and less; while calling on scientific knowledge more and more. They fail to realize that it was God who revealed scientific knowledge to them. They will think they came up with such knowledge on their own.

Regardless of how scientifically advanced mankind become, there are some things which can only be done by God. Science will fail them; however, God will never fail them when they call on Him through Jesus Christ. Nevertheless, instead of calling on Him; they will place their faith in science, technology, and man-made inventions.

In everything, and for everything I will call on the name of the Lord. I will use science, technology, and man-made inventions; but, I will give God the glory, trust in my Savior, and depend on the power of the Holy Spirit. My life and my eternity will be centered on God my heavenly Father through my Lord and Savior Jesus Christ.

Father; I realize that without You, mankind can do nothing. Therefore; all scientific knowledge, modern technology, and man-made inventions come from You. You give us the freedom to choose how to use them; however, they come from You. Therefore, I will give You glory for them, and will use them according to Your will. In Jesus' name I pray; amen.

Jesus my LORD; thank You for giving saints wisdom to know that all things come from You and the Father. Thank You for giving us wisdom to use all things to glorify Your name and to do the work of the Father.

23. Many nations will come against Israel to seek to destroy her

(Luke.21:20) [20] And when ye shall see Jerusalem compassed with armies, then know that the desolation thereof is nigh.

Once Israel becomes a nation again, many will come to hate her, and will eventually seek to destroy her. We will expound on this more in the section of our book entitled, "What nations will be doing". However, for now, there are a few things you need to know concerning Israel.

A. Israel will be one of only a few nations which once existed, ceased to exist, and come into existence again in the last days.

B. Israel will develop into a mighty and prosperous nation.

C. Israel will develop into a military superpower with nuclear weapons.

D. Many nations will hate Israel until eventually all nations come to hate her.

E. Many nations will constantly threaten to destroy Israel.

F. Many nations will constantly seek to divide more and more of her land between her and her enemies.

G. The city of Jerusalem in Israel will be the center of three major religions (Christianity, Judaism, and Muslims).

Because of the increasing hatred for the nation of Israel, God command saints to pray for the peace of Jerusalem. God blesses those who pray for Israel.

(Psalms.122:5-7) 6. Pray for the peace of Jerusalem: they shall prosper that love thee.

While "end time prophecy" effects all nations, kingdoms, and people, keep an eye on Israel. The more hatred grows for Israel, the closer we are to the fulfillment of end time events.

You may not totally understand this but, when You pray for the nation of Israel, God sees it as if you are praying for yourself and for all saints. Israel is God's chosen nation of the Old Testament and of the Tribulation Period; however, today, the church (Christians) are the Israel of God.

> *(Galatians.6:15-16)* ^{15}*For in Christ Jesus neither circumcision availeth any thing, nor uncircumcision, but a new creature.* ^{16}*And as many as walk according to this rule, peace be on them, and mercy,* **and upon the Israel of God***.*

Father; thank You for loving Israel, and thank You for loving saints who are in Your sight the Israel of God. In Jesus' name I pray; amen.

> *Jesus my LORD; as Israel was to God in the Old Testament, the church is to You in the New Testament. We are the Israel of God today. (1st Peter.2:9)* ^{9}*But ye are a chosen generation, a royal priesthood, an holy nation, a peculiar people; that ye should show forth the praises of him who hath called you out of darkness into his marvellous light:* ^{10}*Which in time past were not a people, but are now the people of God: which had not obtained mercy, but now have obtained mercy.*

24. The spiritual eyes of many Jews will be opened and many Jews will accept Jesus Christ as their Messiah (they will become saved)

(Romans.11:25) ²⁵For I would not, brethren, that ye should be ignorant of this mystery, lest ye should be wise in your own conceits; that blindness in part is happened to Israel, until the fulness of the Gentiles be come in.

When you see a dramatic increase of Jews worldwide becoming saved, it should cause you to realize the times of the Gentiles are coming to a close, and Jesus Christ is soon to return.

A. During the times of the Gentiles (the church age, the Dispensation of Grace) many Jews will refuse to believe that Jesus Christ is the Messiah sent from God. They will willingly blind their own eyes to that fact.

B. When the times of the Gentiles is near an end, God will un-blind the minds and hearts of many, many Jews, and they will see that Jesus Christ is the Messiah sent from God. Many will receive Him as Lord and Savior; and will thus become saved.

C. These saved Jews will be called "Messianic Jews".

Today many Jews are accepting Jesus Christ the Messiah at an astonishing rate. While the nation as a whole is still rejecting Jesus, it is amazing to see the vast amount receiving Him into their hearts. Today, many Messianic synagogues are springing up, many orthodox Jews are being converted to Christianity, and many renown Jewish Rabbis are using the Old Testament scriptures to show that Jesus Christ is the Messiah sent from God to save man from their sins.

These are exciting times in Jewish history. We see the prophecies of Old Testament prophets manifesting in our world today. We see God moving in our midst to bring end time events into full manifestation.

Saints of the living God, daily pray for the salvation of Jews and all people. Pray asking God the Father in Jesus' name to prepare you for the events of the last days. Live righteous, pray for others, and serve God with all your heart.

Father; I want to be ready when Jesus' comes. Thank You for working in me and preparing me to be used of You in great, awesome, and amazing ways in these last days. In Jesus' name I pray; amen.

Jesus my LORD; although You were birth into this world through the Jewish race; You and the Father loves all people of all races. Thank you for including gentiles in your eternal plan of salvation.

> *(John.3:16-17)* *[16]For God so loved the world, that he gave his only begotten Son, that whosoever believeth in him should not perish, but have everlasting life. [17]For God sent not his Son into the world to condemn the world; but that the world through him might be saved.*

25. The city of Babylon will be rebuilt
(*or a Babylonian system of government will emerge*)

(Revelation. 18:2-5) ²And he cried mightily with a strong voice, saying, Babylon the great is fallen, is fallen, and is become the habitation of devils, and the hold of every foul spirit, and a cage of every unclean and hateful bird. ³For all nations have drunk of the wine of the wrath of her fornication, and the kings of the earth have committed fornication with her, and the merchants of the earth are waxed rich through the abundance of her delicacies. ⁴And I heard another voice from heaven, saying, Come out of her, my people, that ye be not partakers of her sins, and that ye receive not of her plagues. ⁵For her sins have reached unto heaven, and God hath remembered her iniquities.

A. The old city of **Babylon (*or a Babylonian governmental system*) will be rebuilt** and will eventually become the financial capital of the world.

B. At the end of the Church Age more and more about this city (***or system***) will be discussed in the news.

C. At the beginning of the Tribulation Period, it is believed that the wealth of the world will be transferred to it.

I do not know if this passage of scripture is talking about the literal city of ancient Babylon being rebuilt; or a governmental system that is patterned after the ancient city of Babylon. However, this Babylonian city or system will emerge in the last days. It will be demonically inspired and demonically infested. Although it will be a prosperous city financially, it will be totally against God and against the things of God. It will be a wicked city given over to idolatry, occult practices, and immorality. Many saints will move to that city because of the availability of jobs and career advancements. This city will become so wicked that God will judge it. However, God will warn His people to come out of her before judgment comes. If they do not come out, they will be partakers of the judgment poured out on her.

Whenever God warns you to leave a place, person, or thing; obey Him. Warnings always come before destruction. Do not allow anything (not even your job) to cause you to stay when God says leave.

Father; thank You for revealing end time events to saints. Thank You for warning saints about impending judgment and destruction; and then giving us time to escape. Please help all Your children to hear and obey You. In Jesus' name I pray; amen.

Jesus my LORD; thank You for empowering Your saints to love You, live for You, and serve You, in these last days. Thank You for empowering us to make full proof of our lives, ministries, and service for You.

> *(2nd Timothy.4:5)* *⁵But watch thou in all things, endure afflictions, do the work of an evangelist, make full proof of thy ministry.*

26. The Old Roman Empire will be revised in the form of a consortium of nations coming together to rule the world and will eventually be ruled by the antichrist

(Daniel.8:9-11) ⁹And out of one of them came forth a little horn, which waxed exceeding great, toward the south, and toward the east, and toward the pleasant land. ¹⁰And it waxed great, even to the host of heaven; and it cast down some of the host and of the stars to the ground, and stamped upon them. ¹¹Yea, he magnified himself even to the prince of the host, and by him the daily sacrifice was taken away, and the place of his sanctuary was cast down. (Revelation.13:1-2) ¹And I stood upon the sand of the sea, and saw a beast rise up out of the sea, having seven heads and ten horns, and upon his horns ten crowns, and upon his heads the name of blasphemy. ²And the beast which I saw was like unto a leopard, and his feet were as the feet of a bear, and his mouth as the mouth of a lion: and the dragon gave him his power, and his seat, and great authority.

Many theologians believe that a kingdom will emerge which will eventually be ruled by the antichrist, and will be a resurgent of the old Roman empire. We will expound more on this later in our book in the section entitled, "What nations will be doing".

A. The Old Roman Empire will be revised.

B. Many believe it will be in the form of a consortium of nations coming together to rule the world.

C. During the Tribulation Period the anti-Christ will take over this empire and become its ruler.

All nations of the world are included in Biblical prophecy; even when those nations are not specifically named. Nations and rulers are described in many different ways in scripture. As You grow in the knowledge of eschatology (the study of end time events), you will learn of these descriptions, recognize which nations they are, and what God would have you do concerning these nations. Prophecy and end time events do not have to be a mystery to you. Through prayer, study, and meditation, God will enlighten Your understanding and increase your knowledge.

Father; even in things I do not totally understand, I rejoice in knowing that You are in control, and Your will is being done. You have a plan for nations, and a plan for me. I say; Father Your will be done concerning nations, and concerning me. In Jesus' name I pray; amen.

Jesus my LORD; the greatest kingdom of all is Your Eternal Kingdom. I rejoice that I will forever be a part of that Kingdom. I daily pray to the Father in Your name asking that multitudes will enter into Your kingdom by accepting You into their hearts. *(Colossians.1:12-13)* *[12]Giving thanks unto the Father, which hath made us meet to be partakers of the inheritance of the saints in light: [13]Who hath delivered us from the power of darkness, and hath translated us into the kingdom of his dear Son:*

27. The antichrist will prepare his kingdom

> Rejecting the Kingdom of Christ leads people into the kingdom of the devil through the antichrist. Whose kingdom are you in?

(Daniel.8:9-11) 9And out of one of them came forth a little horn, which waxed exceeding great, toward the south, and toward the east, and toward the pleasant land. (Daniel.8:23-25) 23And in the latter time of their kingdom, when the transgressors are come to the full, a king of fierce *countenance, and understanding dark sentences, shall stand up.* ^{24}*And his power shall be mighty, but not by his own power: and he shall destroy wonderfully, and shall prosper, and practice, and shall destroy the mighty and the holy people.* ^{25}*And through his policy also he shall cause craft to prosper in his hand; and he shall magnify himself in his heart, and by peace shall destroy many: he shall also stand up against the Prince of princes; but he shall be broken without hand.* (Revelation.13:3-5) *And I saw one of his heads as it were wounded to death; and his deadly wound was healed: and all the world wondered after the beast.* ^{4}*And they worshipped the dragon which gave power unto the beast: and they worshipped the beast, saying, Who is like unto the beast? who is able to make war with him?* ^{5}*And there was given unto him a mouth speaking great things and blasphemies; and power was given unto him to continue forty and two months.*

A. When the antichrist kingdom is set up many will not know it is the antichrist kingdom. They will think that a wonderful charismatic leader has emerged to bring peace, joy, and love to the world. People will not know that this is the worst person ever born bringing in the worst earthly kingdom ever.

B. Although he may set up his kingdom before the Rapture, it is believed that he will not be revealed as the antichrist until after the Rapture of the church (i.e. unless the church goes through the Tribulation Period).

When sinful men reject the kingdom of God through Jesus Christ; God gives them the kingdom of the devil through the antichrist. If they do not want the blessings of God; they receive the curses of the devil. If you are not saved, I admonish you to give your heart to Jesus Christ now, because if you do not, you may give yourself to the antichrist later.

Father; please continue drawing people to Jesus Christ by Your Holy Spirit. In Jesus' name I pray; amen.

Jesus my LORD; thank You for receiving me into Your Kingdom. Thank You for giving me everlasting life with You and with the Father.

> *(Psalms 145:13)* *[13] Thy kingdom is an everlasting kingdom, and thy dominion endureth throughout all generations.*

28. The Jews will rebuild their temple and return to animal sacrifice

*(Revelation.11:1-2) ¹And there was given me a reed like unto a rod: and the angel stood, saying, Rise, and measure **the temple of God**, and the altar, and them that worship therein. ²But the court which is without the temple leave out, and measure it not; for it is given unto the Gentiles: and the holy city shall they tread under foot forty and two months.*

A. The Jews will rebuild their temple and return to animal sacrifice.

B. Jews returning to animal sacrifice will show they still have not received Jesus Christ as their Messiah and as the perfect sacrifice for all the sins of man.

> **Nothing but the blood of Jesus Christ the Lamb of God can wash away sin and bring salvation.**

A great sign that we have entered into the last days was Israel becoming a nation again and possessing Jerusalem. A greater sign than that will be when they begin building their temple again. That will signal that we are in the last of the last days. Many of the last day prophecy centers around the temple. The antichrist will defile the temple, and then sit in the temple proclaiming himself to be God.

(2ⁿᵈ Thessalonians.2:3-4) ³Let no man deceive you by any means: for that day shall not come, except there come a falling away first, and that man of sin be revealed, the son of perdition; ⁴Who opposeth and exalteth himself above all that is called God, or that is worshipped; so that he as God sitteth in the temple of God, showing himself that he is God.

Although the Muslim's Dome of the Rock is now sitting on the site where the temple is to be built. Many believe the Dome will be torn down, or the Jews will build the temple beside it. While we are unsure which will happen, we do know they will rebuild their temple and return to animal sacrifices.

Father; what good is it to have a temple if they are not going to do in the temple what You want done. Instead of worshipping the Lamb of God, they will sacrifice lambs from their flock. This will not be pleasing in Your sight. Please continue un-blinding their hearts and mind so they can realize that Jesus Christ is the perfect sacrifice. In Jesus' name I pray; amen.

Jesus my LORD; if it's not about You, it's not about salvation. Salvation is not found in animals, things, or people; it's only found in You. Thank You for being the Lamb of God which takes away the sins of the world.

> *(John.1:29,35)* [29]*The next day John seeth Jesus coming unto him, and saith, Behold* **the Lamb of God**, *which taketh away the sin of the world.* [35]*Again the next day after John stood, and two of his disciples;* [36]*And looking upon Jesus as he walked, he saith, Behold* **the Lamb of God**!

29. The church will be Raptured up into heaven

(1ˢᵗ Thessalonians. 4:14-17) ¹⁴For if we believe that Jesus died and rose again, even so them also which sleep in Jesus will God bring with him. ¹⁵For this we say unto you by the word of the Lord, that we which are alive and remain unto the coming of the Lord shall not prevent them which are asleep. ¹⁶For the Lord himself shall descend from heaven with a shout, with the voice of the archangel, and with the trump of God: and the dead in Christ shall rise first: ¹⁷Then we which are alive and remain shall be caught up together with them in the clouds, to meet the Lord in the air: and so shall we ever be with the Lord.

A. Many believe the Rapture will occur before the antichrist is revealed and before the seven-year peace treaty is signed between the Jews and her enemies. However, not all theologians hold to this view. Many believe the church will go through the Tribulation period.

B. Millions of saints will have disappeared from the earth. There will be no logical or scientific explanation found for why they disappeared.

C. Many sinners will realize saints have been Rapture; however, many others sinners will not know what really happened to these saints.

D. Many sinners will then give their hearts to Jesus Christ for salvation; however, they will have to endure the Tribulation Period.

There is much controversy concerning the time of the Rapture of the church. Regardless of when the Rapture occurs, it will not alter the prophecies of end time events. All things prophesied to happen will happen; however, the church will be on earth when they happen and must endure the Tribulation Period. God will be with them, will bless them, and will bring them through.

Saints must learn to trust God regardless of what time period they live in. Law, Grace, or Tribulation; God is the same God. God keeps His promises, God protects His saints, and God's eternal plan for saints will be accomplished.

Be not dismayed if you are not Raptured before the Tribulation Period; but rejoice that God is with you in every period.

Father; while I look for the Rapture, I will keep my eyes on You. Your will be done concerning the Rapture and concerning end time events. In Jesus' name I pray; amen.

Jesus my LORD; the victory You gives saints works even during the Tribulation Period. If the church is on earth during the Tribulation Period, You will seal us with Your seal of victory, power, and authority. Just as You will seal and protect the 144000 Jewish witnesses, I believe You will do the same for the church if they are on earth during the Tribulation Period. (Revelation.9:4) *⁴And it was commanded them that they should not hurt the grass of the earth, neither any green thing, neither any tree; but only those men which have not the seal of God in their foreheads.*

30. The antichrist will make a seven year peace treaty between Israel and her enemies.

(Daniel.9:27) ²⁷And he shall confirm the covenant with many for one week: and in the midst of the week he shall cause the sacrifice and the oblation to cease, and for the overspreading of abominations he shall make it desolate, even until the consummation, and that determined shall be poured upon the desolate. (Matthew.24:15) ¹⁵When ye therefore shall see the abomination of desolation, spoken of by Daniel the prophet, stand in the holy place, (whoso readeth, let him understand:) (Mark.13:14) ¹⁴But when ye shall see the abomination of desolation, spoken of by Daniel the prophet, standing where it ought not, (let him that readeth understand,) then let them that be in Judaea flee to the mountains: (Daniel.12:11) ¹¹And from the time that the daily sacrifice shall be taken away, and the abomination that maketh desolate set up, there shall be a thousand two hundred and ninety days

A. Many nations will hate Israel and will eventually come and try to destroy her. When nations come to try to destroy Israel the antichrist will arise and somehow make a 7-year peace treaty between Israel and her enemies.

B. Although the peace treaty will be for seven years, the antichrist will break the treaty after 3½ years. He will then defile the temple of the Jews and will try to destroy the Jews. He will offer pig's blood on the altar, and he will sit in the temple and declare himself to be God. The antichrist defiling the temple, offering pig's blood, and proclaiming himself to be God is called "the abomination of desolation."

> **Making a contract with that lying devil never works. It only leads to deception and destruction.**

Never make a pack with the devil because he will not keep it, honor it, nor abide by it. He will break his promises to you (and to everyone else), and he will be the very one seeking to deceive you, defile you, and destroy You.

Father; thank You for making an everlasting covenant with me and all saints through Your Son the Lord Jesus Christ. Thank You for keeping Your promises, fulfilling Your Word, and honoring the blood of Your Son. In Jesus' name I pray; amen.

> *(Titus.1:1-2) ¹Paul, a servant of God, and an apostle of Jesus Christ, according to the faith of God's elect, and the acknowledging of the truth which is after godliness; ²In hope of eternal life,* **which God, that cannot lie**, *promised before the world began;*

Jesus my LORD; the antichrist makes a seven year promise he will not keep; You make an eternal promise that You can not brake. Thank You Jesus for being a promise keeping Savior. I love You my Lord.

31. Much, much, more.

(Daniel.12:4,9) ⁴But thou, O Daniel, shut up the words, and seal the book, even to the time of the end: many shall run to and fro, and knowledge shall be increased. ⁹And he said, Go thy way, Daniel: for the words are closed up and sealed till the time of the end.

A. As we draw closer and closer to the return of Jesus Christ more and more shall be revealed to saints about end time events. Things that saints of yesterday could not perceive or understand will be revealed to saints of today and tomorrow. God will give us greater understanding and greater clarity concerning end time events.

B. Daily pray asking God to open your spiritual heart of understanding so you can know when prophetic events are unfolding before your eyes.

God has not revealed everything which will happen during the last days. Some things He will not share until it's time for them to happen. Saints must grow in hearing the voice of the Holy Spirit in them so they can be informed of impending events which are about to transpire.

Be not surprised when things begin to happen which eschatology teachers have not mentioned. Don't even be surprised when things happen which are not mentioned in the Holy Bible. God have not told it all. He is in control of it all; however, He doesn't tell it all now. When it's time for them to happen, He will reveal it to saint before they transpire.

(Amos.3:7) ⁷Surely the Lord GOD will do nothing, but he revealeth his secret unto his servants the prophets.

Father; please continue developing saints to levels where we can hear Your voice speaking to us revealing unto us things to come, and what to do concerning these things. You do not want saints to be caught unaware nor off guard. Thank You for revealing future events to those who are in tune with Your voice. In Jesus' name I pray; amen.

Jesus my LORD; although many horrific things will transpire during end time events, You have awesome and marvelous plans for Your saints. Before end time events, during end time events, and after end time events, Your blessings and eternal plan shall be fulfilled concerning saints. Lord; I look forward to all You have for saints.

Jesus is LORD

The Physical Creation

> The physical creation refers to the physical things God has created. The earth, its environment, plants, animals, fish, people, outer space, planets, and more; are part of the physical creation.

The Physical creation

Topics of discussions

1. The physical creation will be in travail.

2. A word of warning to saints.

3. Winter.

4. Spring.

5. Summer.

6. Fall.

7. I am not telling it all.

8. God will still be in overall control.

It's about to happen. Not only is it about to happen, it is happening now. Things are now in place which will cause the physical creation to do as prophesied by the prophets of old. These things have been happening, is now happening, and is going to continue happening, but increase in frequency and in severity. If you have not been noticing the environmental conditions of the world lately; it's time to start observing them now.

In this section of our study on eschatology, we will endeavor to reveal to you what I believe the physical creation will go through. The physical creation refers to the physical things God has created. The earth, its environment, plants, animals, fish, people, outer space, planets, and more; are part of the physical creation. While we can not tell it all, we can tell what we believe God has revealed to us through the scriptures. Pray asking God to open Your spiritual eyes of understanding and comprehension.

1. The physical creation will be in travail

*(Romans 8:19-23) 19. For the earnest expectation of the creature waiteth for the manifestation of the sons of God. 20. For the creature was made subject to vanity, not willingly, but by reason of him who hath subjected the same in hope, 21. Because the creature itself also shall be delivered from the bondage of corruption into the glorious liberty of the children of God. 22. **For we know that the whole creation groaneth and travaileth in pain together until now**. 23. And not only they, but ourselves also, which have the firstfruits of the Spirit, even we ourselves groan within ourselves, waiting for the adoption, to wit, the redemption of our body.*

*(1st Thessalonians 5:1-4) 1. But of the times and the seasons, brethren, ye have no need that I write unto you. 2. For yourselves know perfectly that the day of the Lord so cometh as a thief in the night. 3. For when they shall say, Peace and safety; then sudden destruction cometh upon them, **as travail upon a woman with child**; and they shall not escape. 4. But ye, brethren, are not in darkness, that that day should overtake you as a thief.*

The physical creation will be going through such rough changes; the Holy Bible calls them "**travail**." The term "**travail**" refers to the labor pains a woman goes through just before and during the delivery of a baby. Just before the delivery of the baby, her labor pains become **worse and worse**, and increase in **frequency** and **intensity** until the baby is born. First the pains (contractions) are light and do not hurt very badly. However, as the time of delivery draws closer, the pains get worse, and occur more frequently.

Just before Jesus returns, national catastrophes and adverse environmental conditions will manifest more and more. As the time of Christ's return draws nearer and nearer, these things will become worse and worse. Not only will they become worse and worse, they will increase in frequency (they will happen more and more). These national catastrophes and adverse environmental conditions will first happen every once in a while, causing minimal damage. However, as the time of Christ's return draws nearer, these things will increase in frequency and severity (they will happen more often, and cause much more destruction than they previously caused). These things will happen all over the world, and the level of destruction they cause will break all previous records.

If you have noticed earth's environment over the past few years, you would have noticed **hotter summers, colder winters, harsher storms, record breaking temperatures, forest fires, earthquakes, volcanic eruptions, hurricanes, tornados, etc. All of these things (and more) are happening more often and are getting worse and worse.** These and other *Signs of the Times* show the return of Jesus Christ is near.

Father; because things are going to become worse and worse, saints will need your guidance, wisdom, and blessings. Please continue preparing us for the worsening environmental conditions that are about to occur. In Jesus' name I pray; amen.

Jesus my LORD; I am not afraid of what the future holds because I know the One who holds the future. I know You.

2. A word of warning to saints

(1st Timothy.6:7-8) ^{7}For we brought nothing into this world, and it is certain we can carry nothing out. ^{8}And having food and raiment let us be therewith content.

When the earth begins to increase in travail, much damage and destruction will occur to church buildings and to the homes and possessions of saints. Always remember God is more concerned about the people of the church than He is about church buildings. Always remember God is more concerned about you than about your possessions. Make sure you have insurance; do not place great value on physical possessions, and begin to focus more on your relationship with God. During these travailing times your faith and obedience to God will be greatly tested and tried. God will try you and test you to see if you love Him more than you love possessions, people, and things.

To survive in these travailing times

A. Prayer must be a major part of your life. Pray for yourself and others.

B. Faith (trust in God) is something you must have, maintain, and increase in. In these travailing times you must trust God to protect you, provide for you, and to be with you regardless of what may happen around you.

C. You must be obedient to the written Word of God.

D. You must be sensitive to and obedient to the Holy Spirit of God. He will guide you, protect you, and give you wisdom. He will tell you where to go and where not to go. Being sensitive and obedient to Him will make the difference between safety and destruction. To become sensitive to the Holy Spirit, and to increase in your sensitivity to Him, you must always pray, meditate upon the written Word every day and every night, spend quiet time alone with God, acknowledge God in everything, and worship God constantly in spirit and in truth.

E. You must live a righteous lifestyle and quickly repent of any sin you may commit.

F. You must actively serve God inside the church building and outside the church building.

G. You cannot afford to be lukewarm. You must be on fire for Jesus Christ.

H. Learn to walk in the power of God. Expect miracles to manifest in your life, and become more surprised when supernatural things do not happen in your life than when they do happen.

I. Daily increase in your knowledge of the written Word of God.

The environment may travail; however, you don't have to. Trust God. He will bring you through travailing times with peace and contentment in your heart.

Father; You caused me to be birth into this world for such a time as this; even travailing times. Please cause me to fulfill Your divine plan, purpose, and destiny for my life. If writing and educating saints is one of Your purposes for my life, please place this book into the hands of all You want to have it. In Jesus' name I pray; amen.

Jesus my LORD; You fulfilled God's calling on Your life. I, by the power of the Holy Ghost, must fulfill Your calling on my life.

3. Winter

Listed below are some of the things *I believe* will transpire in winter as we draw closer and closer to the return of Jesus Christ.

A. Winters will become worse and worse with record cold temperatures.

B. Record snowfalls will occur more and more.

C. Ice storms will increase in number and in the destruction and devastations they will cause.

D. Places not usually affected by winter's harsh weather will notice that winter conditions have come to them as well. Many people will freeze to death, and many cities (and even nations) will not be able to cope with the extremely cold temperatures they will be confronted with. Also, many cities and nations will not be able to cope with the amount of snowfall they will experience.

E. Many animals will be confused because of the changing weather conditions, and they too will not be able to cope with the changes.

F. **Begin to expect things to happen in winter that have never happened before.** Strange unexplainable things will transpire in such ways that many will be puzzled by them. Scientists will be unable to understand what is happening nor why it is happening.
    1. Just as the people of Noah's days were surprised by water falling out of the sky because it had never rained before the flood (*Genesis 2:5-6*): (rain was a new thing to them) we too, will be surprised by some of the new things that will appear during winter in the last days just before the return of Jesus Christ.

G. There will also be times when winters will be so mild that it will feel like spring, and at times it will feel like summer.

   1. This will not be a good thing because winter helps to control the insect population. Many insects that are usually dormant in winter

(mosquitoes, bees, wasps, etc.) will still be active during winter and will greatly pester people.

2. This will also cause an over-abundance of insects to be produced and will thus show up during the spring and summer seasons. This over-abundance of insects will do great damage to crops and earth's vegetation.

H. During winter, one day there will be record high temperatures, and the next day there will be record low temperatures. Great variations in temperatures will occur instantly and regularly in such ways that everyone will know these things are not normal.

I. There will be other major things transpiring in winter that are not mentioned in this book. I admonish you to study the writings of other notable eschatology teachers to learn more of what will happen to the physical creation in the last days.

Father; please equip saints with generators, food, firewood, and all they will need to be ready for the things which are about to happen during winter. Thank You for solar panels, batteries, and hand operated devices. In Jesus name I pray; amen.

Jesus my LORD; I expect to see Your miracle working power providing for me and others everything we will need to survive winter.

4. Spring

Just as strange and bazaar things will happen during winter, so will strange and bazaar things happen during Spring. Even the spring season of the year will be in travail.

A. Storms in spring will become worse and worse.

B. There will be more thunderstorms than usual.

C. There will be more flooding than ever before.

D. There will also be an increase in tornadoes.

1. These tornadoes will become bigger in size.

2. Their duration will be longer.

3. They will cause more destruction to lives and property than tornadoes of the past.

4. They will develop quicker than tornadoes of the past.

5. They will occur more frequently than ever before.

6. Multiple tornadoes will be produced from one storm super cell.

7. These tornadoes will occur in places that usually do not experience tornadoes.

8. These tornadoes will catch many people unaware and unprepared.

9. These tornadoes will cause much money to be spent on early warning systems.

10. These tornadoes will do things which tornadoes have never done before.

Do not become deceived into thinking the weather conditions on earth are going to get better. Instead of getting better they will get worse and worse. However, trust God (if you are His child) and be not afraid, because He will take care of you. If you are not a child of God, become one **now** by accepting Jesus Christ as your Lord and Savior.

Saints must learn to hear and obey God. When God lays on your heart not to go to work; stay home. When God lays on your heart to leave town for a day, (for no apparent reason); leave. Usually after something bad happens saints will say, "Something told me to go visit my family in another town, but I just didn't do it."

Do not neglect morning prayer each day. After praying, read the Holy Bible and lay still for a few minutes to allow God to speak to your spirit. Most of the time you may not hear God say anything; however, when something bad is about to happen in your life, you will clearly hear God tell you what to do before that bad thing happens.

Do not become so attached to your regular routines that you do not change them **_when you begin to feel uneasy in your heart_**. Whenever you feel uneasy or troubled in your spirit for seemingly no reason, seek God in prayer asking what's about to happen, and what He would have you do *(John.16:13) [13]Howbeit when he, the Spirit of truth, is come, he will guide you into all truth: for he shall not speak of himself; but whatsoever he shall hear, that shall he speak:* and **_he will show you things to come_**.

Father; in these last days, saints must follow the leading of Your Holy Spirit. Please help us to hear Him clearly, and obey Him fully. In Jesus' name I pray; amen.

Jesus my LORD; thank You for opening the eyes of your servants causing them to realize, notice, and perceive that the signs of the time are now manifesting in our world.

5. Summer

(Revelation. 16:8-9) ⁸*And the fourth angel poured out his vial upon the sun; and power was given unto him to scorch men with fire.* ⁹*And men were scorched with great heat, and blasphemed the name of God, which hath power over these plagues: and they repented not to give him glory.*

Be prepared to see, feel, and experience things in summer you never expected to see, feel, or experience. Travailing times will increase with the coming of each summer, and will intensify as the coming of Jesus Christ draws nearer and nearer. Scorching heat is on the way.

A. Summers will become hotter and hotter with record-breaking high temperatures.

B. Great heat waves will occur in different places which usually do not have to deal with such extremely high temperatures.

C. Global warming will become a major issue among men. The north and south poles will begin to change in their geographical composition because of ice melting.

D. There will be major droughts in summer.
   1. Many farms and ranches will be greatly affected and devastated by these droughts, and great demands will be placed on many national leaders by their people to provide appropriate food. These extremely hot summers will also place a strain on utility companies.

E. There will be times when summers will be colder than usual.
   1. The variations in temperatures (being hotter than normal, and being cooler than normal) will be felt in all nations of the world.

F. There will be new, strange, and unusual occurrences taking place during summer. Things that have never happened before will begin to happen.

One of the greatest things saints can do is pray asking God to help them prepare for the travailing times of summer. Saints need to pray for wisdom, discernment, and guidance. Saints need to pray asking God to teach them how to receive a hundred fold return of blessings even during the travailing times of summer.

> *(Genesis.26:1,12) 1.* ***And there was a famine*** *in the land, beside the first famine that was in the days of Abraham. And Isaac went unto Abimelech king of the Philistines unto Gerar. 12.* ***Then Isaac sowed in that land, and received in the same year an hundredfold: and the Lord blessed him***.

Even in the times of famine and travailing summers, God can bless you where you are, even when others are not being blessed. God did it for Isaac, and He will do it for you in these last and evil days.

Father; I rejoice in knowing You are with Your saints even in the scorching times of the end times. In Jesus' name I pray; amen.

Jesus my LORD; even in scorching times I will do Your will, live for You, and serve You.

6. Fall

(Nahum.1:3-4a) *³The LORD is slow to anger, and great in power, and will not at all acquit the wicked: the LORD hath his way in the whirlwind and in the storm, and the clouds are the dust of his feet. ⁴He rebuketh the sea, and maketh it dry, and drieth up all the rivers:*

A. The fall seasons will become worse and worse.

B. Hurricanes and typhoons will increase in number, in size, and in duration.

C. Tsunamis will happen in many coastal areas, and cyclones will occur more and more.

D. Hailstorms will increase in number and in the size of hailstones they will produce. *(Revelation.16:21)* *²¹And there fell upon men a great hail out of heaven, every stone about the weight of a talent: and men blasphemed God because of the plague of the hail; for the plague thereof was exceeding great.*

E. There will be great fluctuations in fall temperatures. At one time, the temperatures will be warmer than usual, and at another time they will be colder than normal.

F. Be not surprised when things begin transpiring during the fall of the year that have never happened before. *(Numbers.16:30)* *³⁰But if the LORD make a new thing, and the earth open her mouth, and swallow them up, with all that appertain unto them, and they go down quick into the pit; then ye shall understand that these men have provoked the LORD.*

When thinking about the devastating things that will occur on earth, also think about the after mass of these things. Power lines down, drinking water polluted, homes and businesses destroyed, shortages of food, shortages of the necessities of life, and much, much more. Think of the lives destroyed, the number of people injured, and how hard life will become after a national disaster. People will rebuild. However, not long after rebuilding, they will experience even worse disasters.

Why do you live where you live? Is it because of the availability of jobs, stores, and schools? Is it because of where your family lives, your company transferred you there, or just because you like that city? If you cannot truly say you live where you live because you truly believe it is where God wants you, then it's time to pray asking God what to do. Start today acknowledging God in all your ways so He can direct your path; and do not rebel against where He is directing you.

Father; thank You for revealing to saints the conditions which are about to transpire on earth, and thank You for protecting us when these events happen. In Jesus' name I pray; amen.

> *(Isaiah.42:9) ⁹Behold, the former things are come to pass, and new things do I declare: before they spring forth I tell you of them.*

Jesus my LORD; I want to be a mighty soldier in Your army in these last days. I want to be a mighty man of valor who fight against the forces of darkness and destroy them to Your glory.

7. I am not telling it all

(Deuteronomy.29:29) ²⁹The secret things belong unto the LORD our God: but those things which are revealed belong unto us and to our children for ever, that we may do all the words of this law.

There are many other things which will happen in our weather conditions that we have not discussed. Our aim is to give you enough information to help you realize that difficult days are ahead, sinners need to get saved, saints need to live right, and servants of the Savior need to get busy serving Him.

God does not always reveal to His servant things that are happening or are about to happen. There are times when God will hide things from His servants.

*(2ⁿᵈ Kings.4:27) 27. And when she came to the man of God to the hill, she caught him by the feet: but Gehazi came near to thrust her away. And the man of God said, Let her alone; for her soul is vexed within her: <u>**and the Lord hath hid it from me, and hath not told me**</u>.*

Inadequate words, limited intelligence, and unrevealed predictions prevents me from telling it all. Ask God to give you greater understanding.

For some unknown reason God does not always tell saints everything that has happened, is happening, and is about to happen. In the scripture above, although the woman's child had died, Elisha would not know about it until he got to the woman's home. God hid that fact from him. Some events God hides from saints until they happen. However, when they happen God equips saints to deal with them just as He equipped Elisha to deal with the woman's deceased child.

When the time is right, God will reveal many, many more events which will transpire during the last days. He will reveal them through the Word, through prophets, or through one's spirit. Daily study the Word, and daily stay in prayer so God can reveal to you events which will transpire during the last days.

Father; even when we do not know all that shall happen, we are still required to trust You. We are to live by faith even in unknown and uncertain times. You will protect us, provide for us, and bless us; even when we do not know all that shall happen in the future. The greatest thing is not knowing the future, it's knowing You. Because I know You; You have my future in Your hands. That brings me great comfort. Thank You my Father for holding me and my future in Your hands. In Jesus' name I pray; amen.

Jesus my LORD; even before I was born into this world, You had my life in Your hands, because You knew I would receive You has my Lord and Savior. You have wonderful plans for my future even though I do not know what they are. Thank You for the wonderful plans You have for me.

> *(Jeremiah.29:11)* *¹¹For I know the thoughts that I think toward you, saith the LORD, thoughts of peace, and not of evil, to give you an expected end.*

8. God will still be in overall control

*(Hebrews.1:3) ³Who being the brightness of his glory, and the express image of his person, **and upholding all things by the word of his power**, when he had by himself purged our sins, sat down on the right hand of the Majesty on high;*

Although our weather conditions (and our world) will get worse and worse, God will still be in control. God will allow bad things to happen, and He will allow the devil, demons, and men to do their thing, however:

A. **God will be the One who says when these bad things can happen.**

> *(Revelation 7:1-3) 1. And after these things I saw four angels standing on the four corners of the earth, holding the four winds of the earth, that the wind should not blow on the earth, nor on the sea, nor on any tree. 2. And I saw another angel ascending from the east, having the seal of the living God: and he cried with a loud voice to the four angels, to whom it was given to hurt the earth and the sea, 3. **Saying, Hurt not the earth, neither the sea, nor the trees, till we have sealed the servants of our God in their foreheads**.*

B. **God will be the One who says how long these bad things can happen.**

> *(Revelation 9:15) 15. And the four angels were loosed, which were prepared **for an hour, and a day, and a month, and a year**, for to slay the third part of men.*

C. **God will be the One who says how bad these bad things can be.**

> *(Revelation 9:5-6) 5. And to them it was given that **they should not kill them, but that they should be tormented five months**: and their torment was as the torment of a scorpion, when he striketh a man. 6. And in those days shall*

men seek death, and shall not find it; and shall desire to die, and death shall flee from them.

D. **God will be the One who says who these bad things can happen to.**

(Revelation 9:3-4) *3. And there came out of the smoke locusts upon the earth: and unto them was given power, as the scorpions of the earth have power. 4. And it was commanded them that they should not hurt the grass of the earth, neither any green thing, neither any tree;* **<u>but only those men which have not the seal of God in their foreheads</u>**.

> **Regardless of what goes on in this world, or in my life; God is still in control. I trust in the controlling power of God.**

It is comforting to know that in the midst of horrible conditions, God is yet in control. Even when He does not keep bad things from happening; He still has overall control of things. He sets the boundaries and limitations of things, and He is the One determining whom these things will affect. However, while He is in overall control, people still have their part in it.

When one becomes saved, he places himself in a position to avoid many of the horrible things that are coming upon the earth. God says these conditions are not to overcome those with His seal upon them. When one refuses to accept Jesus Christ, he refuses the seal. When bad things happen to him, it is really his fault because God gave him a way of escape, through His Son Jesus Christ, but he refused to take it.

Saints, while God will keep you from the bad things mentioned above; He did not promise to keep you from all bad things. God never promised to keep you from all negative situations; however, He did promise to be with you in those things and give you victory over them.

(2nd Corinthians 12:9-10) *9. And he said unto me, My grace is sufficient for thee: for my strength is made perfect in weakness.* **<u>Most gladly therefore will I rather glory in my infirmities,</u>**

> *that the power of Christ may rest upon me. 10. Therefore I take pleasure in infirmities, in reproaches, in necessities, in persecutions, in distresses for Christ's sake: for when I am weak, then am I strong.*
>
> *(1ˢᵗ Peter.5:10) ¹⁰But the God of all grace, who hath called us unto his eternal glory by Christ Jesus, after that ye have suffered a while, make you perfect, stablish, strengthen, settle you.*

Regardless of what's going on around me and in this world, I will look to my God, trust in my God, and obey my God. I know He has an eternal plan and purpose He is accomplishing, even when I don't like if for now, nor understand it. I know that all will turn for my good and for His glory. I know His plans, purposes, and divine destiny is always good, best, and right. His wisdom is impeccable and His ways are pass finding out. He is the all-wise God.

> *(Isaiah.55:6-9) ⁶Seek ye the LORD while he may be found, call ye upon him while he is near: ⁷Let the wicked forsake his way, and the unrighteous man his thoughts: and let him return unto the LORD, and he will have mercy upon him; and to our God, for he will abundantly pardon. **8For my thoughts are not your thoughts, neither are your ways my ways, saith the LORD. 9For as the heavens are higher than the earth, so are my ways higher than your ways, and my thoughts than your thoughts**.*

Father; while I can not always figure out what You are doing, I do want to be a part of it. Although Your ways are higher than my ways; I want to walk in Your ways. I want to be a part of Your eternal plans, purposes, and destiny. Thank You for sending Jesus Christ to make all that, and more, happen for me, and for all who will receive Him. In Jesus' name I pray; amen.

Jesus my LORD; although suffering days are coming upon the whole earth; I know for those who belong to You; the suffering we endure can not be compared to the glory which shall be reveal in us.

(2nd Corinthians.4:17) [17]For our light affliction, which is but for a moment, worketh for us a far more exceeding and eternal weight of glory;

(Romans.8:18) [18]For I reckon that the sufferings of this present time are not worthy to be compared with the glory which shall be revealed in us.

Earthquakes, Mudslides, Volcanic Eruptions, and Other Natural Catastrophes

Earthquakes, Mudslides, Volcanic Eruptions, and Other Natural Catastrophes

Topics of Discussion

1. Earthquakes.

2. Mudslides.

3. Volcanic eruptions.

4. Hot springs and glaciers.

5. Hurricanes, Typhoons, Tsunamis, and Cyclones.

6. Meteor showers.

7. Forest Fires and Wild fires.

8. Floods.

9. Sinkholes.

10. The topography of the entire world will change.

11. Remember it will be like travail. Things will start, stop, and start up again only to get worse.

12. Another reminder.

13. Sin, judgment, and demons.

> **When discerning the *Signs of the Times* do not think of how things use to be, ask God to show you how things are going to be. Things that have never happened are going to happen, and only God can tell you of them.**

While the Holy Bible does not specifically mention mudslides, volcanic eruptions, and other national catastrophes of that nature, they are a part of the shifting and moving of the earth, thus, they fall into the category of travailing events. **Also, as you read the Holy Bible, the Holy Spirit in you will give you illumination and revelation knowledge in such ways that you will understand what will be affected in the last days.**

1. Earthquakes

*(Matthew 24:7) 7. For nation shall rise against nation, and kingdom against kingdom: and there shall be famines, and pestilences, **and earthquakes**, in divers places.*

*(Revelation 16:18) 18. And there were voices, and thunders, and lightnings; **and there was a great earthquake**, such as was not since men were upon the earth, so mighty an earthquake, and so great.*

The shifting and moving of the earth through earthquakes and other natural catastrophes

A. Eearthquakes will increase in number, in severity, and in the amount of destruction they will cause.

B. When one earthquake subsides, another will begin.

C. In many different areas of the world, unexpected earthquakes will occur.

D. Earthquakes will be so strong and so powerful that even our best built buildings will not be able to stand up under the strain of them.

E. The aftershocks of earthquakes will cause as much damage and death as the earthquakes themselves.

F. When it comes to prophetic interpretation of end time events, any and all geological disturbances of the earth such as landslides, mudslides, volcanic eruptions, etc., are in the same category as earthquakes (the earth moving or shifting); therefore, expect them to become worse and worse.

G. Not only do earthquakes occur on land, they also occur in oceans and seas. When there is an earthquake on the ocean floor, it produces an enormous tidal wave which scientists call tsunamis. Expect that to happen more and more; and to become worse and worse as the coming of Jesus Christ draws nearer and nearer.

H. The most powerful and worst earthquakes will happen during the time of the Great Tribulation Period.

I. **I believe** an interesting and new thing is going to transpire concerning earthquakes. While there will be many large earthquakes shaking many cities and counties; there will be extremely powerful earthquakes that will shake only one house or one neighborhood. A seven point earthquake will affect only one person's property; however, it will happen to a vast amount of people one house at a time.

J. **I believe** there will be a powerful earthquake in one block, then skip over a block, and then shake the neighborhood two blocks over.

> *(Revelation 11:13) 13. And the same hour was there **a great earthquake**, and **the tenth part** of the city fell, and in the earthquake were slain of men seven thousand: and the remnant were affrighted, and gave glory to the God of heaven.*

When thinking about earthquakes also think about the consequences which may occur during and after earthquakes. Think of what may happen to a community and town if a dam breaks because of an earthquake. Think about a nuclear reactor and the possible radiation leaks. Think about all the things which will be negatively affected once a powerful and destructive earthquake occurs.

Father; even during earthquakes, Jesus is still my solid rock. In Jesus' name I pray; amen.

2. Mudslides

A. If you have been attentive to the recent events of our world, you would have noticed mudslides have increased around the world.

B. These mudslides have occurred in the United States of America, as well as in other parts of the world. They are increasing in number, and in the severity of the destruction they cause. They are now worldwide problems and they can occur at any time or any season of the year.

As you discern the *Signs of the Times*, you will learn that every facet of our environment will be affected in negative ways. From the seas, to the oceans, to the forests, to the mountains, to the deserts, to the valleys, and to every part of the physical creation of God, catastrophic things will happen. In realizing this fact, it is not hard to see and understand that mudslides are a major part of the earth being in travail.

Do not be surprised when **in the midst of a drought,** suddenly, for some unexplainable reason, the ground becomes extremely moist and mudslides occur. Strange, different, and unexplainable events will begin to happen.

As man increases in sinful activities, the physical creation will increase in travail. Sin has the ability to greatly affect the physical creation in negative ways. Sin has the ability to cause great problems in the lives of those sinning.

Remember it will be travail. These things will happen, and subside for a while. However, they will happen again at a later time. When they happen again, they will be worse than the first time. Mudslides will happen for a while, and then subside for a number of years. After a number of years, they will happen again; however, they will be worse than the first time.

Because a few years have passed, many will forget about them, or think they were just something that happen that year. Many will not equate them with the signs of the times. Those who are saved and have the Spiritual gift of discernment, will know mudslides will happen again, will be worse, and are signs of the times. Do you have spiritual discernment? Do you realize that the mudslides that plagued men a few years ago are a sign of the end times, and will happen again and become worse and worse?

Father; please help saints not to be blind to the signs of the times which are happening in their lives from year to year. Please anoint us with such spiritual discernment that these signs do not go unnoticed by us. In Jesus' name I pray; amen.

Jesus my Lord; not only do I want to notice the signs of the times; I want a word of wisdom concerning what to do in light of these unfolding signs. I want to be prepared for the events of the last days, and I want to prepare others to be ready for these events as well.

3. Volcanic Eruptions

Although I can not find scripture concerning volcanic eruptions, because they are part of the travailing earth, we can not discard them. We must include them as signs of the times. We must include them as end time events.

A. Volcanic eruptions will increase, and cause widespread devastation.

B. Many people will die and many cities, towns, and villages will be destroyed because of volcanic eruptions.

C. Many volcanoes which have laid dormant for years will become active and will eventually erupt.

D. Volcanic eruptions will be extremely powerful and will cover larger areas than man will expect. They will spew lava, ash, and smoke with such power that the lava, ash, and smoke will reach to neighboring states and countries hindering air and ground traffic.

E. Even under water volcanoes (volcanoes under oceans and seas) will begin to erupt and cause great disturbances in oceans and seas. As you begin to hear of these volcanic eruptions, look up, because the coming of Jesus Christ is near.

F. There will be times when, for unexplainable reasons, the earth will suddenly open up and lava and ash will shoot out. This has not happened before; however, **I believe** it will happen as the coming of Christ draws nearer.

While many of the things I am mentioning seems far fetch and outlandish; they are things that will occur. It was far-fetch and outlandish in Lot's days when he told them God was going to rain down fire and brimstone to destroy the city. When Lot told them that was going to happen, they looked at him like many people look at me when they read this book.

> *(Genesis.19:14) 14. And Lot went out, and spake unto his sons in law, which married his daughters, and said, Up, get you out*

of this place; for the Lord will destroy this city. ***But he seemed as one that mocked unto his sons in law***.

Father; only by the leading of Your Holy Spirit can saints escape many of the travailing events of the last days. Your Holy Spirit will lead us out of harm's way, or He will protect us in the midst of what happens around us. Please cause us to become increasingly sensitive to the voice of the Holy Spirit in us. In Jesus' name I pray; amen.

Jesus my LORD; because of how You will protect us during travailing times, sinners will realize they need You and the protection You give. Thank You for drawing sinners to Yourself even during travailing times.

4. Hot springs and glaciers

(Revelation.8:10-11) ⁱ⁰And the third angel sounded, and there fell a great star from heaven, burning as it were a lamp, and it fell upon the third part of the rivers, and upon the fountains of waters; ¹¹And the name of the star is called Wormwood: and the third part of the waters became wormwood; and many men died of the waters, because they were made bitter.

Fountains of waters, including springs, will be negatively affected during travailing times.

A. Even hot springs and glaciers will shoot forth with greater pressure than ever before, many of their waters, however, will be contaminated.

B. Hot springs will begin to develop and form in places where there have never been any before. They will show up in places where homes, businesses, and factories now exist.

While travailing times may change the topography of the fountains of waters; it will not change my love, loyalty, and dedication to God my Father, and to Jesus Christ my Savior.

As long as God keeps me here on earth, I refuse to allow travailing times to keep me from loving God, living for God, and serving God through His Son the Lord Jesus Christ, by the power of the Holy Ghost. I believe God will cause me, and all dedicated saints to rise above the travail of the earth and still accomplish His will on earth.

Even when the antichrist is given power to physically overcome the lives of saints by killing many of them; these saints would rather die loving Jesus, then live physically serving the devil. Not even death could cause them to stop loving God, trusting God, and being committed to God. Is your love, loyalty, and dedication to Jesus Christ unchangeable?

> *(Revelation.13:5-7)* *⁵And there was given unto him a mouth speaking great things and blasphemies; and power was given unto him to continue forty and two months. ⁶And he opened his mouth in blasphemy against God, to blaspheme his name, and his tabernacle, and them that dwell in heaven.* **⁷And it was given unto him to make war with the saints, and to overcome them**: *and power was given him over all kindreds, and tongues, and nations.*

Father; please develop in me a level of dedication that is so great that I would rather die for Jesus Christ, than to live serving the devil. I want to have a level of dedication that's so great that even the travailing times of the earth will not be able to decrease my love, loyalty and devotion to You and to the Lord Jesus Christ. In Jesus' name I pray; amen.

Jesus my LORD; You were dedicated to the Father unto death; even the death of the Cross. I want to be loyal to you unto death; regardless of what type death You chooses for me to die.

> *(Philippians.2:8)* *⁸And being found in fashion as a man, he humbled himself, and became obedient unto death, even the death of the cross.*

5. Hurricanes, Typhoons, Tsunamis and Cyclones

*(Luke 21:25) 25 And there shall be signs in the sun, and in the moon, and in the stars; and upon the earth distress of nations, with perplexity; **the sea and the waves roaring**;*

*(Acts 27:13-14) 13. And when the south wind blew softly, supposing that they had obtained their purpose, loosing thence, they sailed close by Crete. 14. But not long after there arose against it a tempestuous wind, called **Euroclydon**.*

A. Hurricanes, typhoons, and other storms at sea (Euroclydon as they were called in the days of Paul the Apostle) will increase in number and in intensity.

B. Hurricanes will become larger than ever before.

C. Hurricanes will travel greater distances than most scientists will predict.

D. Hurricanes will travel further in land than they normally travel.

E. Hurricanes will hover over land longer than normal.

F. Hurricanes will occur in places where scientists thought it would be impossible for hurricanes to exist.

G. Hurricanes will begin to occur in seasons in which they have never occurred before.

H. Hurricanes will occur even when no tropical depression is detected before-hand.

I. Once Hurricanes reach land, many tornados will be produced from them.

Not only will hurricanes cause major problems but tsunamis, typhoons, and cyclones will become formidable foes for men to contend with just before the return of Jesus Christ.

A. Many coastal towns, villages, and cities will begin to be devastated by unexpected tsunamis.

B. Many tsunamis will occur for unexplainable reasons (scientist will not be able to tell what caused the tsunamis).

C. Storms at sea will be so violent and will happen so suddenly that many great battle ships and merchant ships will be destroyed.

> *(Revelation 8:8-9) 8. And the second angel sounded, and as it were a great mountain burning with fire was cast into <u>the sea</u>: and <u>**the third part of the sea became blood**</u>; 9. And the third part of the creatures which were in the sea, and had life, died; and <u>**the third part of the ships were destroyed**</u>.*

> One of the most amazing things is that more people will become saved during these bad times than became saved during good times. During bad times people realize how much they truly need God.

Our oceans, seas, lakes, and rivers will become more and more unstable, and more and more violent. During the Tribulation Period many of the oceans, seas, lakes, rivers, and streams will turn to blood and to wormwood (they will become greatly polluted and contaminated).

> *(Revelation 8:10-11) 10. And the third angel sounded, and there fell a great star from heaven, burning as it were a lamp, and it fell upon the third part of <u>**the rivers**</u>, and upon <u>**the fountains of waters**</u>; 11. And the name of the star is called Wormwood: <u>**and the third part of the waters became wormwood**</u>; and many men died of the waters, because they were made bitter.*

6. Meteor showers

*(Revelation.6:13) 13. And **the stars of heaven fell unto the earth**, even as a fig tree casteth her untimely figs, when she is shaken of a mighty wind.*

In the last days just before the return of Jesus Christ, expect to see increased meteorite and meteor showers falling into seas, oceans, rivers, lakes, and streams causing great pollution, contamination, and devastations.

While many of these catastrophic environmental events will occur near the end of the church age of the Dispensation of Grace, the greatest and worst catastrophic environmental events will occur during the Tribulation Period. I do pray you will be part of the Rapture; and I pray the Rapture will happen before the Tribulation Period.

If the Rapture does not happen before the Tribulation Period, I pray saints have allowed God to develop them to levels where they can hear the voice of God leading them, guiding them, and giving them instructions on things to do. Only God can keep you from being hurt and/or killed by these meteor showers. Hearing and obeying God will be very important during these times.

(Psalms.32:8) [8] I will instruct thee and teach thee in the way which thou shalt go: I will guide thee with mine eye.

(Isaiah.30:21) [21] And thine ears shall hear a word behind thee, saying, This is the way, walk ye in it, when ye turn to the right hand, and when ye turn to the left.

Sinful, wicked, and abominable living opens the door to many negative and harmful things. Sinful, wicked, and abominable living causes people to stray from under the protective hand of God into the destructive hand of the enemy. Because sin, wickedness, and abominable living will increase more and more in the last days, negative environmental catastrophes will increase more and more in the last days.

(Proverbs.14:34) *³⁴ Righteousness exalteth a nation: but sin is a reproach to any people.*

Saints must always strive by the power of the Holy Ghost to live righteous and godly lifestyles, so God can guide them, provide for them, and protect them, even in the midst of meteor showers.

Father; not even meteor showers can prevent you from being my protector. Regardless of what may happen, I will trust in your protection. In Jesus' name I pray; amen.

Jesus my LORD; in all time periods of human history, saints must remain faithful to You. We must depend on Your Power, obey Your Word, and overcome the forces of darkness. We must be people of love, faith, and worship. Times, situations, and circumstances may change and become worse; however, saints are to remain steadfast, and must mature in You. Thank You for developing saints into what You want them to be, regardless of what time period they live in.

7. Forest Fires and Wild fires

(Revelation 8:7) 7. The first angel sounded, and there followed hail and fire mingled with blood, and they were cast upon the earth: ***and the third part of trees was burnt up, and all green grass was burnt up***.

A. There will be a constant increase in forest fires and wild fires as we draw closer and closer to the return of Jesus Christ. They will increase greatly as we near the end of the Dispensation of Grace; and will reach alarming rates during the Tribulation Period.

B. The destruction caused by these fires will constantly increase year by year.

C. These fires will be a result of lightning strikes, human error, and arson.

The forest fires and wild fires which are raging in this country, and in other countries around the world today, are not that which is spoken of in *Revelation 8:7* (that happens during the Tribulation Period). These present forest fires of today are preludes and previews to the great forest fires which will destroy all green grass and one third of all trees. God is just giving us signs and warnings about the impending evils and judgments that are soon to be unleashed upon this planet.

Are you heeding the signs and warnings God is giving? Are you saved? Are you growing in the knowledge of Jesus Christ? Are you totally living for God? It is time for saints to become real with God; and to constantly increase in Him. He is worthy of such, and He is looking for vessels of honor which will be sanctified and fit for His use.

When forest fires occur in different parts of the world, many homes and possessions of saints will be destroyed. God has not promised to keep saints from all negative and destructive things; however, He promised to be with us in them. Saints are to enjoy the blessings of God while we can. When these blessings are destroyed or taken away; we are to continue trusting God, loving God, worshiping God, and serving God. We are to pray asking God to restore unto us that which we lost.

Never become so attached to physical possessions that you become devastated when they are destroyed or taken away. God has a reason for allowing them to be destroyed or taken away. Therefore, trust Him, and trust that your loss is working together for your good and God's glory.

> (Romans.8:28) ²⁸And we know that all things work together for good to them that love God, to them who are the called according to his purpose.

Father; I love You more than I love things. I love the things You give me, however, my greatest joy comes from knowing You, loving You, living for you, worshiping You, serving You, and praying to You. In Jesus' name I pray; amen.

Jesus my LORD; You have called me for such a season and time as this. Not for the acquisition of things, but for Your service. I refuse to allow possession, people, and things to keep me from loving You, trusting You, and serving You. I may lose possessions and things, but I will never lose You.

8. Floods

How do we know floods will be a problem in the last days? How do we know they will become worse and worse? The book of revelation says nothing about floods being part of the adverse conditions manifesting during the latter days, so how do we know they will be?

> *(John.16:12-13) ¹²I have yet many things to say unto you, but ye cannot bear them now. ¹³Howbeit when he, the Spirit of truth, is come, he will guide you into all truth: for he shall not speak of himself; but whatsoever he shall hear, that shall he speak:* **<u>and he will show you things to come.</u>**

Many of the events of the last days will be revealed to saints by the Holy Spirit who is also called the Spirit of truth. He will show us things to come, and will confirm them to saints. Listed below is some of the things concerning floods in the last days which I believe the Holy Spirit has revealed to me.

A. Flooding will become a major problem in the last days.

B. The waters of oceans, seas, lakes, and rivers, will overflow their banks and flood out many homes, villages, towns, and subdivisions.

C. Floods will also come from an over-abundance of rainfall, and snowfall (as snow melts, massive flooding will occur in some places).

D. Floods will cause massive power outages and will cause bridges and roads to be washed away. Floods will cause farmland and crops to be destroyed. Floods will also cause homes, factories, and commercial buildings to become devastated.

E. Floods will occur in places which have never seen floods before. Places where there are no rivers, streams, or lakes will experience flooding.

F. In some places for unexplainable reasons, the ground will open up and water will spur out causing flooding in many areas.

While floods will be a major problem in the last days; there will not be another world-wide flood like in Noah's day (see Genesis.9:11-17).

God the Father has made so many awesome things available to saints so we can be powerful, authoritative, and unstoppable spiritually. We have the Holy Ghost in us, the name of Jesus Christ, the blood of the Lamb, the written Word of God, the whole armor of God, the fruit of the spirit, the gifts of the Spirit, the word of our testimony, effectual fervent prayers, praise and worship, exceeding great and precious promises, and the victory of the Cross of Christ. It is time for saints to rise to the full level of power God has given us. It is time to overcome the world, the flesh, and the devil; and fully accomplish the will of God in Christ Jesus concerning us in these last days. Nothing, not even floods should be able to stop saints from living for God and serving Him.

Father; thank you for giving saints victory, even in times of flooding. In Jesus' name I pray; amen.

Jesus my LORD; regardless of what happens in this world; by the power of the Holy Ghost, I will press forward in You.

9. Sinkholes

(Revelation 12:16) 16. And the earth helped the woman, and **the earth opened her mouth***, and swallowed up the flood which the dragon cast out of his mouth.*

It is the personal opinion of this writer that one of the unexpected phenomenon which will begin to occur in the last days is the appearance of huge sinkholes. Unpredicted and unexpected sinkholes will appear in different places for reasons unknown to scientists.

> **When things become worse and worse; don't blame God, blame, sin, satan, and mankind.**

Without warning, the ground will suddenly open up and swallow up homes, factories, farms, and forest lands. The opening up of the earth was a judgment from God in the days of old, and I believe it will occur in the future.

(Numbers 16:30-32) 30. But if the Lord make a new thing, and the earth open her mouth, and swallow them up, with all that appertain unto them, and they go down quick into the pit; then ye shall understand that these men have provoked the Lord. 31. And it came to pass, as he had made an end of speaking all these words, **that the ground clave asunder that was under them: 32. And the earth opened her mouth, and swallowed them up***, and their houses, and all the men that appertained unto Korah, and all their goods.*

What has happened will happen again. God will allow the ground to open up causing great sinkholes in different places. Scientists will not be able to explain what caused these sinkholes, nor will they be able to say where and when other sinkholes will occur. Also, sinkholes will become larger and larger.

When I thank about the vast amount of negative things which are about to transpire on this planet, and in all the physical creation, I rejoice that I am a child of God. I rejoice in knowing God will protect me, provide for me, and use me to His glory. He will give me victory over all the attacks of the enemy, and He will cause me to fulfill His divine will for my life.

(2nd Corinthians.2:14) 14Now thanks be unto God, which always causeth us to triumph in Christ, and maketh manifest the savour of his knowledge by us in every place.

> **Because saints are God's children, instead of experiencing His wrath during the time of wrath; they will experience His grace, protection, and provision.**

Father; I must cry loud and spare not telling people Jesus is the only way of salvation and deliverance. I must show sinners Your love, mercy and power. In Jesus' name I pray; amen.

Jesus my LORD; in the midst of all the negative travailing things transpiring in these last days, I must remember that You are in control. I have no need to fear because You are in control.

10. The topography of the entire world will change

(Revelation.6:14) *[14]And the heaven departed as a scroll when it is rolled together;* **and every mountain and island were moved out of their places**.

(Revelation.8:7) *[7]The first angel sounded, and there followed hail and fire mingled with blood, and they were cast upon the earth:* **and the third part of trees was burnt up, and all green grass was burnt up**

Things on earth will be dramatically changed. The topography of this planet will experience enormous changes just before and during the Tribulation Period. Every mountain and island will be moved out of its place, 1/3 of all trees will be burned, and all green grass will be burned. Streams, lakes, seas, and oceans will be polluted. Some will even turn into the blood of a dead man, while others will be turned into wormwood.

(Revelation.16:3) *[3]And the second angel poured out his vial upon the sea;* **and it became as the blood of a dead man**: *and every living soul died in the sea.*

(Revelation.8:10-11) *[10]And the third angel sounded, and there fell a great star from heaven, burning as it were a lamp, and it fell upon the third part of the rivers, and upon the fountains of waters; [11]And the name of the star is called Wormwood:* **and the third part of the waters became wormwood;** *and many men died of the waters, because they were made bitter*

During the Great Tribulation Period, this world would have changed so dramatically that it will look nothing like it does today. Catastrophic changes will occur, and nothing will remain the same. Stars will fall from heaven, the sun and moon will black out from time to time, and demons will infest the earth causing pain, destruction, and death. The only things which will not change is God Himself, and His written Word.

While the greatest changes will occur during the Tribulation Period, many of these changes are happening now in our world today. Climate change, forest fires, floods, earthquakes, and man's destruction of rainforest and other national habitats is altering the topography of our world today. These changes will only become worse as time passes, and will reach their fullness during the Tribulation Period. Saints must begin noticing the changes in our world, and realize these changes are signs of the times manifesting in our midst. Signs which are pointing to the coming Tribulation Period, and to the soon return of Jesus Christ.

Father, the topography of the earth may change; however, Your mercy, grace, and love will never change. They will forever be available to all who will receive them by receiving Jesus Christ. In Jesus' name I pray; amen.

> *Jesus my LORD; Thank You for (Malachi.3:6) ⁶For I am the LORD, I change not; therefore ye sons of Jacob are not consumed.*

11. Remember it will be like travail. Things will start, stop, and start up again only to get worse

Always remember these signs are like birth pains. They will start and then stop. Therefore, be not surprised when these things happen and then stop for a while. Things may be really bad one year, and then for the next two years nothing may seem to happen. Just remember and be assured these travailing birth pains will happen again, and they will eventually get worse and worse.

> *(Jeremiah.12:5) . ⁵If thou hast run with the footmen, and they have wearied thee, then how canst thou contend with horses? and if in the land of peace, wherein thou trustedst, they wearied thee, then how wilt thou do in the swelling of Jordan?*

If in these peace, calm, and good times we can not to stand strong for the Lord Jesus Christ, how shall we stand in travailing times? It is not surprising that many will fall away in the end times. Because they were not faithful, committed, and dedicated when all was going well; they will not be faithful, committed, and dedicated when all hell breaks loose.

Everyday, saints should reaffirm their love for God, commitment to God, and service for God. Saints need to spend good times preparing for bad travailing times. Saints should be fortifying their faith, increasing their commitment, and strengthening their resolve in Christ. We need to stay filled with the Holy Ghost, stay in constant prayer, and stay in praise and worship to God. We must grow in our love for God, in the knowledge of God, and in the power of God.

> *(Revelation.16:12-14) ¹²And the sixth angel poured out his vial upon the great river Euphrates; and the water thereof was dried up, that the way of the kings of the east might be prepared. ¹³And I saw three unclean spirits like frogs come out of the mouth of the dragon, and out of the mouth of the beast, and out of the mouth of the false prophet. ¹⁴For they are the spirits of devils, working miracles, which go forth unto the kings*

of the earth and of the whole world, to gather them to the battle of that great day of God Almighty.

In a time of physical wars between nations, and spiritual war against God; God caused you to be born in such a time and season as this. He has a special plan and purpose for you to fulfill. Count yourself privileged and bless to be used of God to prepare people for the world changing events which are about to happen on this earth.

Father; in these changing times; You need unchanging saints. You need those who will be steadfast, unmovable, and always abounding in the work of the Lord. Please continue developing me into a steadfast, unmovable, child of Yours. In Jesus' name I pray; amen.

Jesus my LORD; I have decided to follow You; no turning back; no turning back.

> *(1ˢᵗ Corinthians.15:58)* ⁵⁸*Therefore, my beloved brethren, be ye stedfast, unmoveable, always abounding in the work of the Lord, forasmuch as ye know that your labour is not in vain in the Lord.*

12. Another reminder

Although we have endeavored to teach you many things about the soon return of Jesus Christ, and about discerning the *Signs of the Times*, if you do not study the written Word of God for yourself, you will not get a full understanding. If you do not study for yourself, these things will still seem somewhat of a mystery to you, and you will remain confused and frightened.

> **When you study the Word for yourself; God will reveal to you things He has not included in this book. He wants to give you greater revelations of end time events.**

> *(Acts 17:10-12) 10. And the brethren immediately sent away Paul and Silas by night unto Berea: who coming thither went into the synagogue of the Jews. 11. These were more noble than those in Thessalonica, in that **they received the word with all readiness of mind, and searched the scriptures daily, whether those things were so**. 12. Therefore many of them believed; also of honourable women which were Greeks, and of men, not a few.*

Only after studying the written Word of God daily can a saint get an understanding of its contents, and then believe what it says. The Word of God has the power to enlighten a saint's understanding, and touch his heart in such powerful ways that he will be able to comprehend the things written therein.

> *(Psalms.119:130) 130. **The entrance of thy words giveth light; it giveth understanding unto the simple**.*

Not only does God's Word give you enlightenment and understanding, it draws you closer and closer to God. It causes you to get to know God in ways you could never know Him without constant and daily study. It strengthens your heart, increases your love for God, and elevates your service for God to higher levels. There are more benefits to studying the Word for yourself than we could ever mention in this small book.

The more you study for yourself the more useful you will become in the kingdom and service of God. In these last days of travailing times and increasing evil; God needs strong, powerful, and committed soldiers to combat the forces of darkness. He need warriors of the Word who will whip the devil, destroy demons, and overpower unclean spirits.

Father; here am I, send me. Whatever You need me to do, I make myself available to You. I purpose to study Your Word, live Your Word, and grow in Your Word so You can use me as You please. In Jesus' name I pray; amen.

Jesus my LORD; because of who You are, and because of all You have done, I want to love You, live for You, and serve You. You are worthy of my greatest service. I daily and constantly give it to You.

13. Sin, judgment, and demons

(Revelation.18:5-6) ⁵For her sins have reached unto heaven, and God hath remembered her iniquities. ⁶Reward her even as she rewarded you, and double unto her double according to her works: in the cup which she hath filled fill to her double.

The reason the earth will be in travail is because of man's constant increase in sinful activity. Increasing sinful activities:

A. Causes the earth to travail and increase in travailing.

B. Causes man to come from under God's protecting hands.

C. Causes the judgment of God to come upon the earth.

D. Causes the devil and demons to bring great evil and destruction on earth.

Saints, if you are involved in sinful activities; it's time to repent now. It's time to give your heart totally to Jesus Christ in righteous, holy, and godly living. You do not want to be a contributing cause of God's judgment coming upon the earth.

Sadly; many of God's chosen servants will not repent nor turn from their sins. Just as the prophets and priest were corrupt in Ezekiel's days when God had to judge Judah; many pastors, preachers, and saints are corrupt today.

(Ezekiel.22;25-26) ²⁵There is a conspiracy of her prophets in the midst thereof, like a roaring lion ravening the prey; they have devoured souls; they have taken the treasure and precious things; they have made her many widows in the midst thereof. ²⁶Her priests have violated my law, and have profaned mine holy things: they have put no difference between the holy and profane, neither have they showed difference between the unclean and the clean, and have hid their eyes from my sabbaths, and I am profaned among them.

Even in these last days, many of the women preachers (prophetess) will be corrupt.

> *(Revelation.2:21-22)* *²⁰Notwithstanding I have a few things against thee, because thou sufferest that woman Jezebel, which calleth herself a prophetess, to teach and to seduce my servants to commit fornication, and to eat things sacrificed unto idols. ²¹And I gave her space to repent of her fornication; and she repented not. ²²Behold, I will cast her into a bed, and them that commit adultery with her into great tribulation, except they repent of their deeds. ²³And I will kill her children with death; and all the churches shall know that I am he which searcheth the reins and hearts: and I will give unto every one of you according to your works.*

Father; in the midst of corruption in the world and in the church; please anoint me, empower me, and motivate me to live holy, righteous, and godly in Your sight. Please lead me not into temptation; and please deliver me from evil. And while You are doing that for me; do it for all Your true dedicated servants. In Jesus' name I pray; amen.

Jesus my LORD; holiness is who You are; and holiness is what You require of Your saints. I purpose by the power of the holy Ghost to live a holy, righteous, and godly lifestyle.

Strange Occurrences In Outer Space

Strange Occurrences In Outer Space

Topics of Discussion

A. Strange occurrences in outer space.

B. UFOs in the sky.

C. Will the moon really turn to blood, and will the sun and moon really stop shining?

If you were to talk to astrologists today, they would confirm the fact that strange things are now starting to happen in earth's atmosphere, and in outer space. With the invention of new and stronger telescopes, space probes, and space shuttles; scientists and astrologers are now able to see clearly what's going on in outer space. Astrologers now are able to report on these strange occurrences using pictures, videos, and other modern means of technology.

We are living in thrilling times. The prophets of the Old and New Testament would have loved to have lived in the days in which we now live. They would love to be able to see what we are about to see transpire in our world. It was, no doubt, exciting to hear the prophets prophesy about these things, but it's more exciting seeing these things manifest before our very eyes today.

Father; as we embark on this part of our study; please give me and the readers understanding and illumination according to Your will. In Jesus' name I pray; amen.

Jesus my LORD; be glorified in this section of our study.

1. Strange occurrences in outer space

*(Matthew 24:29) 29. Immediately after the tribulation of those days shall **the sun be darkened, and the moon shall not give her light, and the stars shall fall from heaven, and the powers of the heavens shall be shaken**:*

*(Luke 21:25) 25. And there shall **be signs in the sun, and in the moon, and in the stars**; and upon the earth distress of nations, with perplexity; the sea and the waves roaring;*

*(Joel 2:30-32) 30. And **I will shew wonders in the heavens** and in the earth, blood, and fire, and pillars of smoke. 31. **The sun shall be turned into darkness, and the moon into blood, before the great and the terrible day of the Lord come**. 32. And it shall come to pass, that whosoever shall call on the name of the Lord shall be delivered:*

*(Revelation 8:12) 12. And the fourth angel sounded, and **the third part of the sun was smitten, and the third part of the moon, and the third part of the stars;** so as the third part of them was darkened, and the day shone not for a third part of it, and the night likewise.*

As we draw closer and closer to the soon return of Jesus Christ, strange and bizarre things will begin happening in the air and in outer space. Newspaper articles and television news programs will constantly report on stories about strange occurrences in earth's atmosphere, and unexplainable phenomenon in outer space.

These strange things will begin happening just before the Tribulation Period begins, and will intensify during the Tribulation Period. These things will be so bizarre and so different that many will be able to tell God is up to something. Scientist will seek to come up with scientific explanations as to why these things are transpiring; however, the saints of God will know these things are the *Signs of the Times* being fulfilled.

In *Acts.2:19* it says *"And I will shew wonders in heaven above."* For centuries men have looked into the heavens and seen the same things. Now that we are drawing closer and closer to the return of Jesus Christ, men will look into the heavens and see strange things they have never seen before. **I believe** that some of these strange things will include, but not be limited to:

A. Unusual cloud formations.

B. Changes in the jet stream.

C. Many stars deteriorating.

D. Many stars will merge together to form larger ones.

E. Black holes forming in outer space.

F. New galaxies suddenly appearing.

G. Increased meteor showers.

H. Some stars will be changing their color.

I. The light of many stars will grow dim.

J. Great unexpected and unexplainable explosions.

K. Unidentifiable dust clouds and dust formations.

L. The sun will grow dark.

M. The moon will turn into bright red blood.

N. Unidentifiable objects moving through space.

O. Unrevealed things (Things not revealed until the time of the end).

P. Etc.

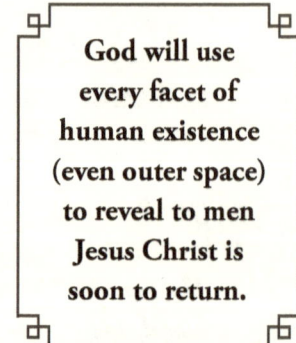

God will use every facet of human existence (even outer space) to reveal to men Jesus Christ is soon to return.

2. UFOs in the sky

*(Revelation 9:1-3) 1. And the fifth angel sounded, and **<u>I saw a star fall from heaven unto the earth</u>**: and <u>**to him**</u> was given the key of the bottomless pit. 2. And **<u>he</u>** opened the bottomless pit; and there arose a smoke out of the pit, as the smoke of a great furnace; **<u>and the sun and the air were darkened by reason of the smoke of the pit</u>**. 3. And there came out of the smoke locusts upon the earth: and unto them was given power, as the scorpions of the earth have power.*

Just before the return of our Lord and Savior Jesus Christ, when men look into the sky, they will see many unidentifiable objects. In seeing these things, they will think extra celestial beings are coming to earth. However, what they will see are:

A. Meteor showers.

B. Planets changing shapes, forms, and colors.

C. Cosmic explosion in outer space.

D. God allowing **demonic spirits** to come down to earth. (God will allow some people to see these demonic spirits when usually demonic spirits are invisible to men).

E. Angels preaching the everlasting gospel.

> *(Revelation. 14:6-7) [6]And I saw another angel fly in the midst of heaven, having the everlasting gospel to preach unto them that dwell on the earth, and to every nation, and kindred, and tongue, and people, [7]Saying with a loud voice, Fear God, and give glory to him; for the hour of his judgment is come: and worship him that made heaven, and earth, and the sea, and the fountains of waters.*

While there are no such things as spacemen and spaceships, when sinners see demonic spirits falling to earth from outer space, the changes that will take place in outer space, and angels preaching the everlasting gospel; they will call them extra celestial beings traveling about the galaxies.

Do not be surprised at the reports you hear about things going on in the heavens. Just remember the best way to explain them is to know what the Holy Bible says would happen in outer space during the last days, and then realize the things going on are nothing but the *Signs of the Times* being fulfilled.

From planets, to demons, to angels; many awesome, amazing, and astonishing things will transpire in the heavens above our heads. Only the spiritually mature will understand what's really going on.

Father; thank You for telling saints things to come. When they eventually show up, we will have true understanding of what's going on. Thank You for giving us understanding. In Jesus' name I pray; amen.

Jesus my LORD; when I look up into the heaven, I am looking for Your coming.

> *(1st Thessalonians.4:16-17) 16For the Lord himself shall descend from heaven with a shout, with the voice of the archangel, and with the trump of God: and the dead in Christ shall rise first: 17Then we which are alive and remain shall be caught up together with them in the clouds, to meet the Lord in the air: and so shall we ever be with the Lord.*

3. Will the moon really turn to blood and will the sun and the moon really stop shining?

*(Acts 2:19-20) 19. And I will shew wonders in heaven above, and signs in the earth beneath; blood, and fire, and vapour of smoke: 20. **<u>The sun shall be turned into darkness, and the moon into blood, before that great and notable day of the Lord come</u>**:*

*(Revelation 8:12) 12. And the fourth angel sounded, **<u>and the third part of the sun was smitten, and the third part of the moon, and the third part of the stars; so as the third part of them was darkened, and the day shone not for a third part of it, and the night likewise.</u>***

Some people wonder if God is speaking symbolically or literally. I believe God is speaking literally and the sun will literally turn dark, the stars will literally stop shining, and the moon will literally turn to blood. Some believe God was speaking symbolically thus the moon will just turn a bright red color but not literally into blood.

If God is speaking literally concerning the sun and stars, He is speaking literally concerning the moon. To doubt this is to doubt the power of God. God is so powerful that He is well able to turn the moon into blood.

Even when we are unsure of the meaning of a passage of scripture, we can be sure that God is in control, and His will shall be done. Rather it's symbolic or literal, what God has prophesied to happen will happen.

(Isaiah.14:24) [24]The LORD of hosts hath sworn, saying, Surely as I have thought, so shall it come to pass; and as I have purposed, so shall it stand:

Even when You do not totally understand all things, know all things, or hear of all things, you are still to trust God, believe God, and obey God. You are to love God, live for God, and serve God. Worship Him, acknowledge Him, and adore Him. He has everything in control. All will turn out as He says.

Father; even in the darkness of my none understanding, I will trust You. In Jesus' name I pray; amen.

Jesus my LORD; all things happening during end time events, are included in Your eternal plans of salvation. We must first go through these things before eternity future can begin.

Blind to the Signs

While Everything is Changing; It Will Seem Nothing is Changing

While Everything is Changing, It Will Seem Nothing is Changing

(2nd Peter 3:3-4) *3. Knowing this first, that there shall come in the last days scoffers, walking after their own lusts, 4. And saying, Where is the promise of his coming?* **for since the fathers fell asleep, all things continue as they were from the beginning of the creation.**

Topics of Discussion

A. The devil knows the end is coming.

B. Deceived by the devil.

C. Delusions from God.

It is interesting and befuddling to me how people can know what the Holy Bible says, see it manifesting in their sight, but yet deny it is true. They are being deceived into hell if they do not repent, and become saved. Daily pray asking God to un-blind the minds of those who are deceived so they can repent once they see.

There are some; however, who see and still will not repent. Because they refuse to repent, God will help them believe a lie. It is a very dangerous and damning thing to purposely reject truth when you see it. Are you rejecting the truth of the Word, and the signs of the times which are manifesting in Your sight?

Father; thank You for delivering me from spiritual deception and from spiritual darkness. In Jesus' name I pray; amen.

Jesus my LORD; I can see that salvation is only of You.

1. The devil knows the end is coming

> *(Revelation 12:12) 12. Therefore rejoice, ye heavens, and ye that dwell in them. Woe to the inhabiters of the earth and of the sea! for the devil is come down unto you, having great wrath, because* **he knoweth that he hath but a short time**.

The devil and demons know the end is coming, and one day they will end up in eternal torment in The Lake of Fire. That is why they once asked Jesus if He was coming to torment them before the time.

> *(Matthew 8:29) 29. And, behold, they cried out, saying, What have we to do with thee, Jesus, thou Son of God?* **art thou come hither to torment us before the time**?

Things the devil and demons know:

A. **They know the end is coming.** *(1ˢᵗ Peter.4:7a) ⁷But the end of all things is at hand: be ye therefore sober, and watch unto prayer.*

B. **They know hell was made for them.** *(Matthew.25:41) ⁴¹Then shall he say also unto them on the left hand, Depart from me, ye cursed, into everlasting fire, prepared for the devil and his angels:*

C. **They know time is winding up and they only have a short time left.** *(Revelation.12:12) ¹²Therefore rejoice, ye heavens, and ye that dwell in them. Woe to the inhabiters of the earth and of the sea! for the devil is come down unto you, having great wrath, because he knoweth that he hath but a short time.*

D. **They know they will soon end up in The Lake of Fire to be tormented forever and ever; and even forever more.** *(Revelation.20:10) ¹⁰And the devil that deceived them was cast into the lake of fire and brimstone, where the beast and the false prophet are, and shall be tormented day and night for ever and ever.*

E. **They know Jesus Christ is coming again quickly.** *(Revelation.22:20)*
   ²⁰*He which testifieth these things saith, Surely I come quickly. Amen. Even so, come, Lord Jesus.*

   Because the devil and demons know these things:

1. They will become very angry and will show great wrath.

2. They will increase their war against saints of God.

3. They will seek to continually deceive sinners into believing that nothing is happening thus they do not need to become saved.

4. They will strive to take as many people to hell with them as they can.

   Because saints know these things

1. We increase in our love for God

2. We live righteous, holy, and godly lifestyles.

3. We increase in praying for the lost.

4. We increase in serving God.

5. We increase in testifying to sinners inviting them to receive Jesus Christ now.

6. We increase in fighting against the devil and defeating him.

Father; because the times are short and Jesus is soon to return, I purpose to press forward by the power of the Holy Ghost to accomplish Your will. In Jesus' name I pray; amen.

2. Deceived by the devil

As we draw closer and closer to the return of Jesus Christ the devil will increase his efforts to take as many to hell with him as he can. He will work harder, longer, and more tenaciously at seeking to keep sinners unsaved. Because he is a great deceiver; his greatest tool will be deception. One of his greatest deceptions will be deceiving men about the true meaning of the *Signs of the Times* that are happening around them.

> **I will listen to and believe God. I will not listen to and believe the lies of the enemy. Who are you listening to and believing?**

While everything is changing the devil is going to deceive sinners in such ways they will not know anything is going on. He will deceive sinners into believing that the things happening on earth are normal things which are supposed to happen. He will tell them we have always had floods, hurricanes, storms, and natural disasters. He will tell them the things going on now are nothing new or different. Many will believe him and thus be damned for eternity.

The devil will also deceive people by giving them different reasons for these disasters. He will tell them these changes in the weather and in earth's environment are the results of:

1. Global warming (climate change).

2. The depletion of the Ozone.

3. Man's pollution.

4. Other physical reasons.

The devil will then make people think these are problems men can correct, and eventually scientists will fix these problems. He will tell them men will overcome these problems and make this world a better world. He will tell people this is not leading up to the end of the world, and they have nothing to worry about. However, regardless of what scientist do, things will continually get worse and worse until Jesus Christ comes.

Another thing the devil will do is allow others to think the end of the world is near, but it's not because of the coming of Jesus Christ. He will make them think this world will just blow up, and there is nothing anyone can do about it. He will say all things come to an end, and this world is no exception. He wants people to think that the end of this world has nothing to do with God, or with the coming of Jesus Christ.

The devil will also work to cause people of different religions to think their messiah is coming to save the world. However, "their messiah," that the devil will cause them to believe in, and look for, is not the Lord Jesus Christ. It will really be the antichrist. He will tell them their messiah will deliver the world from its worsening conditions and make this world a utopia on earth. The devil will try to do all he can to divert people's attention away from the soon return of Jesus Christ.

Father; regardless of what the devil does, I will allow the light of Jesus Christ to shine brighter, and brighter through me. In Jesus' name I pray; amen.

Jesus my LORD; I purpose to spread the truth of Your gospel as far and wide as I can, by the power of the Holy Ghost.

3. Delusions from God

If a person wants to remain a sinner and remain in sin, God will allow him to do so. God will also help him to do so. In the last days, God will send sinners strong delusions.

(2nd Thessalonians 2:7-12) 7. For the mystery of iniquity doth already work: only he who now letteth will let, until he be taken out of the way. 8. And then shall that Wicked be revealed, whom the Lord shall consume with the spirit of his mouth, and shall destroy with the brightness of his coming: 9. Even him, whose coming is after the working of Satan with all power and signs and lying wonders, 10. And with all deceivableness of unrighteousness in them that perish; because they received not the love of the truth, that they might be saved. 11. **_And for this cause God shall send them strong delusion, that they should believe a lie_**: *12. That they all might be damned* **_who believed not the truth, but had pleasure in unrighteousness_**.

> **God will allow to be deceived only those who want to be deceived. If you receive truth; God will give you truth. If you receive lies; God will allow lies to come your way.**

Because people refuse to believe God, God will allow them to believe the lies of the devil, and to be deceived by the devil. However, before God allows the devil to deceive them, God has made available to them.

A. His Holy written Word.

B. The *Signs of the Time*.

C. The testimonies of saints.

D. The move of the Holy Spirit upon their conscience.

E. Television and radio ministries.

F. National and international ministries.

G. A worldwide holiday that celebrates the birth of His Son Jesus Christ.

H. A worldwide holiday that celebrates the death and resurrection of His Son Jesus Christ.

I. And so much, much more.

After doing all of this, **and more**, if people still want to believe the devil, God will allow them to do so. If they have pleasure in acts of unrighteousness, and do not want the truth of God, God will turn them over to their pernicious ways, and send them strong delusions so they can believe the lies of the devil.

Who will you believe, God or the devil?

Father; I purpose to overcome the lies and deceptions of the devil by speaking the light of truth into the lives of sinners. I will tell them of Your love, grace, and salvation through Jesus Christ. Truth overcomes lies for those who have a humble and submissive heart. Please lead me to those who possess a humble and submissive heart. In Jesus' name I pray; amen.

Jesus my LORD; I rejoice in knowing You are the way the truth and the life.

> *(John. 14:6) ⁶Jesus saith unto him, I am the way, the truth, and the life: no man cometh unto the Father, but by me.*

The *Signs of the Times* are found only in the Holy Bible because it is the only true Holy Book from God

(Isaiah. 46:9-10) ⁹Remember the former things of old: for I am God, and there is none else; I am God, and there is none like me, ¹⁰Declaring the end from the beginning, and from ancient times the things that are not yet done, saying, My counsel shall stand, and I will do all my pleasure:

There is no book in all existence like the Holy Bible. It is the only book that comes from God, and it is the only book that contains the true *Signs of the Times*. God gave us this Holy book to reveal to men that He is the only true and living God, and to show us that no one can declare the end from the beginning but Him.

> **How can I not realize God's Word is true? I daily see the truth of God's Word manifesting through the signs of the times.**

The devil, demons, and men try to imitate the prophetic ability of God. Speculation, guess work, manipulation, educated guesses, and conjecture is what men, demons, and the devil do when they try to predict the future. Sometimes their guesses are correct, **but most of the time their guesses are incorrect.** God is the only one who gives a multitude of prophecies, and whose prophecies are always 100% correct. If you do not believe that, just look at the *Signs of the Times* around you and then read the Holy Bible. That should make you a believer.

The devil is good at making educated guesses and deceiving manipulations. The devil will look at the prophecies God gives, and then he will give prophecies close to what God says, but he will alter the outcome of the prophecy to fit a conclusion (and an interpretation) he wants. The devil is also good at manipulating circumstances in such ways that he deceives people into thinking he (or those he is working through) is giving true predictions and prophecies. Are you one of those deceived by the devil and his lies?

The enemy will even work miracles to deceive people into hell. *(Revelation.16:13-14)* *¹³And I saw three unclean spirits like frogs come out of the mouth of the dragon, and out of the mouth of the beast, and out of the mouth of the false prophet. ¹⁴For they are the spirits of devils, working miracles, which go forth unto the kings of the earth and of the whole world, to gather them to the battle of that great day of God Almighty.*

If a miracle does not glorify God through His Son the Lord Jesus Christ; the miracle worker is not of God. Do not follow miracles, follow Jesus. When you follow Jesus, miracles will follow You. *(Mark.16:17-18)* *¹⁷And these signs shall follow them that believe; In my name shall they cast out devils; they shall speak with new tongues; ¹⁸They shall take up serpents; and if they drink any deadly thing, it shall not hurt them; they shall lay hands on the sick, and they shall recover.*

Father, the enemy can imitate and manipulate prophecies; but he can never imitate or manipulate Your love and Your grace. It was Your love and grace through Jesus Christ that drew me to You. Thank You my Father for love and grace. In Jesus' name I pray amen.

Jesus my LORD; the greatest miracle in all existence is You.

What Religions Will Be Doing Just Before The Return Of Jesus Christ Part. 1

What Religions Will Be Doing Part. 1

Topics of discussion

1. Many saints and churches will become rich in this world but will be of no use to Christ.

2. Many saints will be filled with the Holy Ghost which will empower them to live righteous lifestyles and serve God with power.

3. Many saints will preach the gospel of Jesus Christ around the world.

4. Many people and churches will drift away from the true teachings of Jesus Christ and the written Word of God.

5. Many churches will have a form of godliness but deny the power thereof.

6. False Christs and false prophets with false religions will come on the scene just before the return of Jesus Christ.

7. Religious leaders will try to form a one-world religion.

The thing which sets Christianity above all religions is that Christianity is not just a religion; it is a relationship of love and grace between God and man. God extends His love and grace; men receive it by receiving Jesus Christ. Once they receive Jesus Christ they enter into an eternal relationship with God. God becomes their Father forever; Jesus Christ becomes their bridegroom forever, and the Holy Ghost indwells them forever.

Father; thank You that salvation is a love thing. In Jesus' name I pray; amen.

Jesus my LORD; thank You for saving me and others.

1. Many saints and churches will become rich in this world but will be of no use to Christ

*(Revelation 3:14-19) 14. And unto the angel of the church of the Laodiceans write; these things saith the Amen, the faithful and true witness, the beginning of the creation of God; 15. I know thy works, that thou art neither cold nor hot: I would thou wert cold or hot. 16. So then because **<u>thou art lukewarm</u>**, and neither cold nor hot, I will spue thee out of my mouth. 17. Because **<u>thou sayest, I am rich, and increased with goods, and have need of nothing; and knowest not that thou art wretched, and miserable, and poor, and blind, and naked</u>**: 18. I counsel thee to buy of me gold tried in the fire, that thou mayest be rich; and white raiment, that thou mayest be clothed, and that the shame of thy nakedness do not appear; and anoint thine eyes with eye salve, that thou mayest see. 19. As many as I love, I rebuke and chasten: be zealous therefore, and repent.*

The seventh and last church addressed in the book of Revelation (chapter three) is the church of the Laodiceans. Because it was the last church addressed in this series of seven churches, many believe it represents the final condition of the church just before the Tribulation Period begins.

> **If you can not truly say you are on fire for Jesus Christ; you can truly say you are distasteful to Jesus Christ.**

A. This last day Laodicea church was lukewarm. They were not hot and on fire for God. Can you truly say you are on fire for Jesus Christ in every area of your life?

B. This last day Laodicea church was more concerned about financial prosperity and making a living, than about growing in their faith. Which is more important to you, faith or finances?

C. This last day Laodicea church was filled with pride over their physical possessions.

D. This last day Laodicea church was devoid of faith towards God. They trusted in their jobs, money, technology, medical science, other people, and their possessions; however, they had little to no trust in God.

E. This last day Laodicea church was devoid of serving God. They went to church; however, they were not actively engaged in any works of service in or outside the church.

> **Do you have enough faith to produce what you do not have money to buy? Do you trust more in your Father than in your finances?**

F. This last day Laodicea church was wretched, miserable, poor, blind, and naked in the sight of God, however, they did not know it (they were deceived about their true spiritual condition).

G. This last day Laodicea church had put Jesus outside the church (He was standing outside knocking seeking to come in).

> *(Revelation 3:20) 20. Behold, I stand at the door, and knock: if any man hear my voice, and open the door, I will come in to him, and will sup with him, and he with me.*

One must remember that Jesus was talking to the church and not sinners when He made the statement of standing at the door and knocking. Have you placed Jesus out of your church, home, job, lifestyle, etc.? What areas of your life is Jesus knocking on trying to get in?

2. Many saints will be filled with the Holy Ghost which will empower them to live righteous lifestyles and serve God with power

*(Acts 2:17-18) 17. And it shall come to pass in the last days, saith God, **I will pour out of my Spirit upon all flesh**: and your sons and your daughters shall prophesy, and your young men shall see visions, and your old men shall dream dreams: 18. And on my servants and on my handmaidens **I will pour out in those days of my Spirit; and they shall prophesy**:*

While a lot of negative things will happen in the religious realm just before the return of Jesus Christ, there will also be a lot of positive things happening among true Christians. One of the positive things that will happen is many saints will be filled with the Holy Spirit. Because of increased demonic activities, religious deception, and all of the other adverse things which will occur on earth, saints of God will need to walk in greater power and authority. Saints in the last days will cry out to God asking Him to fill them with His Holy Spirit

> **One Holy Ghost filled saint can accomplish more for Christ than a church full of none Holy Ghost filled saints.**

*(Luke 11:13) 13. If ye then, being evil, know how to give good gifts unto your children: **how much more shall your heavenly Father give the Holy Spirit to them that ask him**?*

The fact that many saints will be filled with the Holy Spirit will show up in their lifestyles and in the mighty things God will do through them. Sinners will be able to tell that the things these saints are doing can only be accomplished by God working in them. Daily pray asking God the Father in the name of Jesus to fill You with the Holy Ghost, and to keep You filled with the Holy Ghost.

I want to live a lifestyle that is so powerful that all can tell I am filled with the Holy Ghost. By the way I talk, by the love I show, and by the Power I demonstrate, all will know I am filled with the Holy Ghost. I want everyone to know that I have been with Jesus, and that the Spirit of God is in me.

> *(Acts.4:13)* [13]*Now when they saw the boldness of Peter and John, and perceived that they were unlearned and ignorant men, they marvelled; and they took knowledge of them, that they had been with Jesus.*

Saints must advance to levels where we allow God to works signs, wonders, and mighty deeds through us to the glory of Christ.

> *(Acts.4:29)* [29]*And now, Lord, behold their threatenings: and grant unto thy servants, that with all boldness they may speak thy word,* [30]*By stretching forth thine hand to heal; and that signs and wonders may be done by the name of thy holy child Jesus.*

Father; In these last days, saints must live in, and flow in all the power You have made available to us. Please anoint us to glorify You through signs, wonders, and mighty deeds. In Jesus' name I pray; amen.

Jesus my Lord; I want everyone to know I have been with You.

3. Many saints will preach the gospel of Jesus Christ around the world

*(Matthew 24:14) 14. **<u>And this gospel of the kingdom shall be preached in all the world</u>** for a witness unto all nations; and then shall the end come.*

In these last days, sinners, false prophets, the devil, demons, the antichrist, the false prophet, and those of other religions will do all they can to stop the spread of the gospel of Jesus Christ; **but they will fail.** This Gospel of the kingdom of God through His Son Jesus Christ will reach into the ears of all people all over the world.

From missionaries going around the world on the mission fields, to radio, to television, to gospel literature, to Christian websites, etc., the gospel of Jesus Christ will spread around the world. There will be Christian books, Christian movies, Christian plays, and other Christian programs that will be used to spread the gospel to all nations. However, the dominate ways in which the gospel will spread are:

> **If you can not become involved in preaching the gospel around the world; you can become involved in praying for those who do.**

A. Through preachers as they preach the gospel.

B. Through missionary work.

C. Through Christian media.

D. **Through the godly lifestyles and testimonies of Christians** as they come in contact with people in their homes, schools, jobs, stores, and throughout the world

E. Eventually, angels will be involved in preaching the everlasting gospel.

Because the time will be short, and because the days will be evil, the most important thing will be getting the gospel to sinners. We will face great opposition, nevertheless, we must, by the power of the Holy Spirit prevail. Instead of letting up, backing up, and slacking up; saints must step up in spreading the gospel around the world.

What are you doing to help preach the gospel of Jesus Christ around the world? Are you praying? Are you supporting? Are You witnessing? Just what are You doing?

Father; as we draw nearer and nearer to the soon return of Jesus Christ; please empower many saints to touch the lives of more and more people with the gospel. In Jesus' name I pray; amen.

Jesus my LORD; I daily look for opportunities to spread Your gospel as far as I can by the power of the Holy Ghost. I look for Your Divine favor, Your Divine provisions, and Your Divine Power to so manifest in my life that I can constantly increase in touching people with Your gospel. I look for these things and more for myself, and for all Your dedicated servants.

> *(Matthew.28:18-20)* [18]*And Jesus came and spake unto them, saying, All power is given unto me in heaven and in earth.* [19]*Go ye therefore, and teach all nations, baptizing them in the name of the Father, and of the Son, and of the Holy Ghost:* [20]*Teaching them to observe all things whatsoever I have commanded you: and, lo, I am with you alway, even unto the end of the world. Amen.*

4. Many people and churches will drift away from the true teachings of Jesus Christ and the written Word of God

*(2nd Timothy 4:3-4) 3. For the time will come when **they will not endure sound doctrine**; but after their own lusts shall they heap to themselves teachers, having itching ears; 4. And **they shall turn away their ears from the truth**, and shall be turned unto fables*

*(2nd Thessalonians 2:3) 3. Let no man deceive you by any means: for that day shall not come, **except there come a falling away first**, and that man of sin be revealed, the son of perdition;*

> You are either drawing closer to God or closer to the devil. Who are you drawing closer to?

In the last days just before the return of Jesus Christ, there will be a great drifting away from the true teachings of the Word of God. Three major things will occur, (1) **people** will begin drifting away from what they know the Bible says and will turn to false teachings and false religions. (2) Many **churches** will drift further and further away from the godly doctrines taught in the Word of God. They will develop their own doctrines, or try to mix the truth of God's Word with compromises and falsehoods. (3) **Many saints** will know what the Word says; however, they will live sinful lifestyles anyway. They know the truth of God but willingly live in sin.

Reasons why false doctrines will creep in

A. Many people want a religion that will allow them to do as they please, therefore they reject the righteous standards our God demands in His written Word.

B. Many people want to hold on to their sins and still try to worship God.

C. Many people seek spiritual and physical power, but not God's way.

D. Many people are ignorant of the true teachings of the Holy Bible. They depend on what others say instead of learning what the Holy Bible truly says. Because they don't know the Word, they are drawn into falsehoods and sin.

E. Many people fear persecution. All who live righteous in Christ Jesus will suffer persecution. They do not want to be persecuted by family, friends, co-workers, and society thus they will compromise their conviction for Christ and accept a compromising socially acceptable gospel.

> **Do you obey the truth of the Word you already know? If you will not do what you know to do; you are opening up yourself to receive false doctrine.**

F. Many people are trying to escape the message of being judged by God. They want a gospel where everyone will be accepted into heaven and will not be judged for their sins nor for their earthly lifestyle. They don't want to have to give an account to God for how they lived.

G. Many churches and religious leaders will seek to merge all religions into one universally acceptable religion.

H. Many of the new translations of the Holy Bible will be filled with false teachings and thus will lead many astray.

As we draw closer to the coming of Jesus Christ, many new modern day translations of the Bible will emerge. Many of these translations will include doctrines, phrases, and words which will alter the true meaning of the Word of God.

A. If the translation you use deny the virgin birth of Jesus Christ; discard it.

B. If the translation you use deny that Jesus Christ is the only begotten Son of God; discard it.

C. If the translation you use deny that Jesus Christ is God in a human body; discard it.

D. If the translation you use deny salvation **only** by grace through faith in the finished work of Jesus Christ on the Cross; discard it.

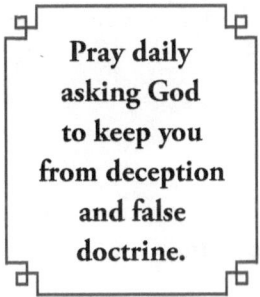

Pray daily asking God to keep you from deception and false doctrine.

E. If the translation you use espouse another way of salvation other than through Jesus Christ (if it says there are other ways you can be saved); discard it.

F. If the translation you use deny that Jesus Christ, the Son of God is coming again; discard it.

G. If the translation you use deny that you should love everyone, live a righteous holy lifestyle, and live by faith in the power of God, discard it.

Sin, false doctrine, powerless saints, the cares of this world, and the deceitfulness of riches, will be major reasons many will fall and drift away from God. Many will become lukewarm and thus distasteful to Jesus Christ because they are so busy working to make a living, they slack up in prayer, worship, service, and living a righteous lifestyle.

> *(Revelation.3:15-19) ^{15}I know thy works, that thou art neither cold nor hot: I would thou wert cold or hot. ^{16}So then because thou art lukewarm, and neither cold nor hot, I will spue thee out of my mouth. ^{17}Because thou sayest, I am rich, and increased with goods, and have need of nothing; and knowest not that thou art wretched, and miserable, and poor, and blind, and naked: ^{18}I counsel thee to buy of me gold tried in the fire, that thou mayest be rich; and white raiment, that thou mayest be clothed, and that the shame of thy nakedness do not appear; and anoint thine eyes with eyesalve, that thou mayest see. ^{19}As many as I love, I rebuke and chasten: be zealous therefore, and repent.*

One of the most dangerous things that will happen to saints in the last days is that many will decrease in their love for Jesus Christ. Many will unknowingly slack up in loving Jesus as they should. They will no longer love going to church, worshiping Jesus, serving Jesus, and living for Jesus.

> *(Revelation.2:2)* ⁴*Nevertheless I have somewhat against thee, because thou hast left thy first love.*

When you do anything for Jesus and not love Him and others as you should, you and your service are nothing in His sight (see 1st Corinthians.13:1-3).

Father; I do not want to drift from loving You and the Lord Jesus Christ; and I do not want to drift from the truth of Your written Word. I want to be true to You in love and in doctrine. In Jesus' name I pray; amen.

Jesus my LORD; thank You for being love, and for being the truth. Thank You for all You are, and all You do. I trust in the Holy Spirit to keep me loving You and others; and to keep me in sound true doctrine.

5. Many churches will have a form of godliness but will deny the power thereof

(2nd Timothy 3:1-5) 1. This know also, that in the last days perilous times shall come. 2. For men shall be lovers of their own selves, covetous, boasters, proud, blasphemers, disobedient to parents, unthankful, unholy, 3. Without natural affection, trucebreakers, false accusers, incontinent, fierce, despisers of those that are good, 4. Traitors, heady, highminded, lovers of pleasures more than lovers of God; 5. **Having a form of godliness, but denying the power thereof***: from such turn away.*

In the last days just before the return of Jesus Christ many churches will have a form of religious worship and a godly facade, but there will be no power to change lives, no power to break the bondage of the devil people are living in, and no power to see souls won to Jesus Christ. There will be no power to see miracles performed, people healed, and God meeting people's needs in miraculous ways. In a time when the miracle working power of God will need to be seen the most, most saints will deny God's power.

> **A powerless religion is a Christ-less religion. The Christ I serve has all power. He made that power available to saints through the Holy Ghost.**

Saints deny the power of God by denying that God still works miracles. They will say that miracles, the gifts of the Spirit, and the anointing with oil passed away when the last apostle died. Because of these and other excuses, they will cause saints to do things by their own ability and intelligence, and not by the power of Almighty God.

God tells saints to turn away from such churches. God wants saints to turn to churches and preachers that teach saints how to trust in and live in the power of God.

(1st Corinthians 2:4-5) 4. And my speech and my preaching was not with enticing words of man's wisdom, but in demonstration of the spirit and of power: 5. **_That your faith should not stand in the wisdom of men, but in the power of God._**

Father; I must allow You to infuse me with the Power needed to live for You, serve You, and accomplish Your will for my life. I must possess the Power to pray life changing prayers, praise in ways that cause Your glory to manifest in my life, and battle victoriously against the forces of darkness.

> Do you have the power to live holy, and to faithfully serve God?

Father; You are depending on me to allow Your Power to flow through me; others are depending on me to allow Your Power to flow through me, and the lost are depending on me to allow Your Power to flow through me. Please increase in allowing Your Power to flow through me and through all Your servants. In Jesus' name I pray; amen.

Jesus my LORD; because of the things which must be accomplished to Your glory in these last days, I refuse to do anything which will prevent Your Power from flowing through me. I purpose to be an empowered servant of Yours to Your glory. I trust the Holy Spirit to cause that to happen for me and for all Your servants.

6. False Christs and false prophets with false religions will come on the scene

*(Matthew 24:11, 24) 11. And **<u>many false prophets shall rise</u>**, and shall deceive many. 24. For **<u>there shall arise false Christs,</u>** and **<u>false prophets</u>**, and shall shew great signs and wonders; insomuch that, if it were possible, they shall deceive the very elect.*

In the last days just before the return of Jesus Christ, many will come claiming they are the Christ. Through false teachings, deceiving miracles, and lying wonders, they will deceive many into following them. These false Christs will prosper from their followers, and will eventually lead their followers into perdition (eternal separation from God) and destruction (being cast into the Lake of Fire). The only ones who will not be deceived by these false Christs are the elect of God (those who are saved). **It is very important to become saved and to know your Holy Bible so well that you will be able to discern truth from error and deception.**

> I live righteous, teach truth, and obey God to show me that I am a real and true servant of the Lord Jesus Christ. To live sinfully, teach wrong, and constantly rebel show I am a false prophet.

Reasons why false prophets will fool so many people

A. Many people will be unsaved and thus susceptible to the deceptions of the devil and his false prophets.

B. Many people will enjoy the pleasures of sin so much that they will refuse to turn to God.

C. Many people will not know the written Word of God. Ignorance of the Word leads to being deceived by the devil and his false prophets.

D. Many people will be deceived by the false signs, lying wonders, and deceiving miracles false prophets work.

E. Many people will want the prosperity these false prophets promise to give them.

F. Many people will not want the true Christ thus they will accept and receive false Christs.

G. Many people will desire to hear new and profound things more so than hearing the truth of God's Word.

> **If you do not want the real; and if you will not be the real; God will give you the false Christ; and He will allow you to be a false Christian**

H. Many people will be too caught up into the cares of this world to be concerned about knowing and loving God.

I. Many people will know what the Holy Bible says but will willingly disobey it anyway.

J. Many people will know what the Holy Bible says but will be deceived into thinking God is telling them to do something different than what's written in the Word. They fail to realize that God will never tell them to do anything that is in violation of the written Word.

Marks of a false prophet, preacher, teacher, and Christ

A. They glorify themselves and not the Lord Jesus Christ.

B. They have people looking more to them than to God.

C. Instead of making people holier and godlier they cause people to increase in sinful things.

D. They talk of salvation without Jesus being **the only way** to obtain it.

E. They say people can get to God without Jesus Christ.

F. They say all religions are different roads to heaven.

G. They try to imitate true preachers and teachers. They have the same preaching and teaching styles, they dress the part, and they talk of love and salvation but not through Jesus Christ.

H. They use the Holy Bible but interpret it wrong.

I. They place other writings equal to or above the Bible.

J. They have sin in their lives and cannot cease from their sins (some are homosexuals, alcoholics, drug addicts, fornicators, adulterous, etc.).

K. They deny that Jesus Christ is God manifest in the flesh.

L. They deny the virgin birth of Jesus Christ.

M. They deny Jesus is coming again

> **They may deceive others; but they will never deceive Jesus. He knows they are false.**

God never intended for people to place their hope and trust in religious leaders, He wants people to place their trust in Him through His Son Jesus Christ. When religious leaders violate the written Word of God people are not to follow them.

It is time to be real with Jesus Christ. Saints must denounce the hidden things of dishonesty, wickedness, and hypocrisy. We must live lives in such ways that all will know we are truly in the faith.

> **After reading this; and you remain a false prophet; it is no one's fault but yours.**

(2nd Corinthians. 13:5) 5Examine yourselves, whether ye be in the faith; prove your own selves. Know ye not your own selves, how that Jesus Christ is in you, except ye be reprobates?

Father; You have been too good to me for me to turn against You with sin and false doctrine. Instead of driving people away from You, I want to draw them to You through Jesus Christ. Thank You for using me for people's salvation, not their damnation. In Jesus' name I pray; amen.

Jesus my LORD; You are too wonderful, awesome, and amazing for me to betray You by being false and by spreading false doctrine. Your love for me and the grace You have given me makes me love You more, worship You more, and live for You more. All the days of my life; and even forever more, I want to be real with You.

7. Religious leaders will try to form a one-world religion

(Revelation 13:14-15) 14. And deceiveth them that dwell on the earth by the means of those miracles which he had power to do in the sight of the beast; saying to them that dwell on the earth, that they should make an image to the beast, which had the wound by a sword, and did live. 15. And he had power to give life unto the image of the beast, that the image of the beast should both speak, **<u>and cause that as many as would not worship the image of the beast should be killed</u>***.)*

In the last days just before the return of Jesus Christ, many religious leaders will try to form a one-world religion. They will outlaw all religions and then demand all people (religious people and nonreligious people) to worship the beast and the image of the beast.

When they outlaw all religions they will seek to kill anyone who refuses to worship the beast and the image of the beast. Christianity, the Catholic religion, Judaism, Muslims, the Confucius religion, Pantheism, the new age religion, and all religions will be outlawed. If anyone seeks to remain in those outlawed religions it will be a capital offence (people will be killed for trying to stay in those religions).

This one world religion will be so powerful that it will seek to cause all people to receive:

A. **The mark of the beast in their right hands or foreheads;** or,

B. **The name of the beast in their right hands or foreheads;** or,

C. **The number of his name (666) in their right hands or foreheads.**

(Revelation 13:16-18) 16. And he causeth all, both small and great, rich and poor, free and bond, to receive a mark in their right hand, or in their foreheads: 17. And that no man might

*buy or sell, save he that had **the mark**, or **the name of the beast**, or **the number** of his name. 18. Here is wisdom. Let him that hath understanding count the number of the beast: for it is the number of a man; and his number is **Six hundred threescore and six**.*

Without the **mark**, or the **name**, or the **number** of his name, people will not be able to sell anything nor buy anything. All who refuse to receive the mark, the name, or the number; those in authority will seek to kill them. We are living in a time when saints of God must make a bold declaration to the world that we are serving the Lord Jesus Christ. We then must remain loyal to Christ against all odds. We can no longer compromise our conviction or waiver in our love and loyalty to Christ. With all of the religious deceptions coming into our world, we must let the world know we serve the only true and living God through His Son Jesus Christ. We must let the world know we will stand for Him, and Him only. We will stand for Jesus Christ by the power of the Holy Ghost unto the end.

What Religions Will Be Doing Just Before The Return Of Jesus Christ Part. 2

What religions will be doing Pt.2

Topics of discussion

8. The devil and demons will manifest their power and presence.

9. The world will hate and persecute Christians.

10. Israel will rebuild the temple and return to animal sacrifices.

11. The devil and the antichrist will make war against the saints of God.

12. Many saints will be strong and do exploits

13. I have not told it all.

> *(2nd Peter.3:17) ¹⁷Ye therefore, beloved, seeing ye know these things before, beware lest ye also, being led away with the error of the wicked, fall from your own stedfastness.*

The time is coming; and now is, when the enemy of our souls will do all he can to draw saints away from the faith. Saints must, by the power of the Holy Ghost, determine to remain steadfast, unmovable, and to always abound in the things of the Lord. We must daily and constantly guard against allowing anyone or anything to cause us to fall from our steadfastness. As we draw closer and closer to the return of Jesus Christ, the pressure placed on saints will become greater and greater. However, because the Greater One lives in us, we are well able to stand and persevere to the glory of God.

8. The devil and demons will manifest their power and presence

(Revelation 13:13-14) 13. <u>**And he doeth great wonders, so that he maketh fire come down from heaven on the earth in the sight of men, 14. And deceiveth them that dwell on the earth by the means of those miracles which he had power to do**</u> *in the sight of the beast; saying to them that dwell on the earth, that they should make an image to the beast, which had the wound by a sword, and did live.*

(Revelation 16:13-14) 13. And I saw three unclean spirits like frogs come out of the mouth of the dragon, and out of the mouth of the beast, and out of the mouth of the false prophet. 14. <u>**For they are the spirits of devils, working miracles**</u>*, which go forth unto the kings of the earth and of the whole world, to gather them to the battle of that great day of God Almighty.*

In the last days just before the return of Jesus Christ, God will allow the devil and demons to exercise great power, to perform many miracles, and to work many amazing deeds. Because of these mighty miracles and amazing deeds, many people will be led astray.

One of the greatest miracles they will perform is the miracle of financial prosperity. In the last days the antichrist will be empowered by the devil to cause craft to prosper. This will keep people from looking to God and cause people to look to him.

(Daniel 8:24-25) 24. <u>**And his power shall be mighty, but not by his own power**</u>*: and he shall destroy wonderfully, and shall prosper, and practise, and shall destroy the mighty and the holy people. 25.* <u>**And through his policy also he shall cause craft to prosper**</u> *in his hand; and he shall magnify himself in his heart, and by peace shall destroy many: he shall also stand up against the Prince of princes; but he shall be broken without hand.*

A description of the power that God will allow the devil and demons to perform

A. The power to deceive.

B. The power to work wonders and miracles.

C. The power to prosper people financially.

D. The power to win wars.

E. The power to influence people.

F. The power to govern and lead nations.

G. The power to speak eloquently.

H. The power to be worshiped by the unsaved.

I. The power to make an image speak.

J. The power to call down fire from heaven.

Because the devil and demons will manifest such power in the last days. There are certain things saints must do.

A. Saints must learn to walk in the power of God so all the world can see that true power and miracles come from God.

B. Saints must pray for sinners and saints not to be deceived by the powers of darkness.

C. Saints must live righteous lifestyles so all can see the blessings God pours out on those who are His.

D. Saints must learn the Word of God so well they will be able to recognize the devil and demons when they come with their deceptive lying miracles.

E. Saints must learn to stop and cancel out the works of the devil and his demons. We are to do this in the name of Jesus, by the power of the Holy Spirit, and through quoting the Word of God with faith and authority.

F. Saints must learn to cast the devil and demons out in the name of Jesus.

G. Saints must show the world that the greatest power is the power of Christian love. Loving God above all things and loving others as one love themselves.

A. **Saints must realize they have more power than the devil.**

> (1st John 4:1-3) 3. And every spirit that confesseth not that Jesus Christ is come in the flesh is not of God: and this is that spirit of antichrist, whereof ye have heard that it should come; and even now already is it in the world. 4. Ye are of God, little children, and have overcome them: because **greater is he that is in you, than he that is in the world**.

B. **Saints must realize they can stop the power of the devil.**

> (Acts 13:8-11) 8. But Elymas the sorcerer (for so is his name by interpretation) withstood them, seeking to turn away the deputy from the faith. 9. **Then Saul, (who also is called Paul,) filled with the Holy Ghost**, set his eyes on him, 10. And said, O full of all subtilty and all mischief, thou child of the devil, thou enemy of all righteousness, wilt thou not cease to pervert the right ways of the Lord? 11. And now, **behold, the hand of the Lord is upon thee, and thou shalt be blind, not seeing the sun for a season**. And immediately there fell on him a mist and a darkness; and he went about seeking some to lead him by the hand.

C. **Saints must realize they can overcome the power of the devil.**

> (Isaiah 54:17) 17. **No weapon that is formed against thee shall prosper**; and every tongue that shall rise against thee

in judgment thou shalt condemn. This is the heritage of the servants of the Lord, and their righteousness is of me, saith the Lord.

D. Saints must realize they can deliver people from under the power and influence of the devil.

*(Jude 1:20-23) 20. But ye, beloved, building up yourselves on your most holy faith, praying in the Holy Ghost, 21. Keep yourselves in the love of God, looking for the mercy of our Lord Jesus Christ unto eternal life. 22. And of some have compassion, making a difference: 23. **And others save with fear, pulling them out of the fire;** hating even the garment spotted by the flesh.*

We are living in a time when saints must rise up and live in the fullness of all God has made available to them through the redemptive work of the Lord Jesus Christ.

Father; I am believing You that I and all Your servants will utilize all You have given us so we can defeat the powers of the devil, and deliver people from them. In Jesus' name I pray; amen.

Jesus my LORD; thank You for giving us victory over all the powers of the enemy. I purpose to daily live in that victory.

9. The world will hate and persecute Christians

*(Mark 13:9,12-13) 9. But take heed to yourselves: for <u>**they shall deliver you up to councils; and in the synagogues ye shall be beaten**</u>: and ye shall be brought before rulers and kings for my sake, for a testimony against them. 12. Now the brother shall betray the brother to death, and the father the son; and children shall rise up against their parents, and <u>**shall cause them to be put to death**</u>. 13. And ye <u>**shall be hated of all men for my name's sake**</u>: but he that shall endure unto the end, the same shall be saved.*

*(Revelation 12:17) 17. And the dragon was wroth with the woman, <u>**and went to make war with the remnant of her seed, which keep the commandments of God, and have the testimony of Jesus Christ**</u>.*

Persecution of saints will increase more and more as we draw nearer to the coming of Jesus Christ. Today, in many nations of the world, it is against the law to be a Christian, to preach the gospel of Jesus Christ, and to worship in Jesus' name. In many nations today, to become saved is a capital offence that is strictly enforced.

In America (which is supposed to be a Christian nation), prayer has been taken out of public schools, the Ten Commandments have been taken out of court houses, and the law separates God from the state. In America, as well as in other nations of the world, it is becoming more and more unpopular to be a Christian. As the coming of Christ draws nearer, people of the world will despise, ridicule, hate, persecute and kill Christians.

> *(Proverbs.24:10)*
> *[10]If thou faint in the day of adversity, thy strength is small.*
>
> **If you are standing strong for Jesus Christ today; you will stand strong for Him during persecution.**

A few things that **I believe** will happen in America as the coming of Jesus Christ draws nearer are:

A. Christians will lose more and more of their religious freedoms.

B. The preaching of the gospel will become more and more restricted until it eventually becomes totally forbidden and illegal.

C. Christian media (radio, television, internet, newspapers, newsletters, magazines, etc.) will be heavily monitored and censored until they are totally forbidden and outlawed.

D. Many church tax exempt status will be revoked and heavy taxation of churches will begin.

E. The right to wear Christian clothing and Christian symbols in work places, in schools, and in public places will be taken away.

F. It will become more and more difficult to be a Christian.

G. More governmental control will come over churches dictating what they must and must not do. Many churches will be mandated to perform same-sex marriages, remove religious symbols (such as crosses), and allow preachers from other religions to regularly address the congregations.

The only way you can rest assured that you will be able to stand strong in the times of persecution is if you are standing strong now. Are you standing strong for Jesus today? Do you stand strong against the persecution you receive at work and from friends and family members? Do you stand strong against the temptations the devil brings your way? If you want to stand strong, you must constantly grow in your love for God and in your knowledge of who God is. The more you know God, the more you will stand strong for Him.

> (Jeremiah. 12:5) *⁵If thou hast run with the footmen, and they have wearied thee, then how canst thou contend with horses? and if in the land of peace, wherein thou trustedst, they wearied thee, then how wilt thou do in the swelling of Jordan?*

> *(Daniel 11:32) 32. And such as do wickedly against the covenant shall he corrupt by flatteries: but* **_the people that do know their God shall be strong, and do exploits_**.

Also daily ask God to keep you filled with His Holy Spirit so you can stand strong by His power in these last days.

> *(John.15:18) ¹⁸If the world hate you, ye know that it hated me before it hated you. ¹⁹If ye were of the world, the world would love his own: but because ye are not of the world, but I have chosen you out of the world, therefore the world hateth you. ²⁰Remember the word that I said unto you, The servant is not greater than his lord. If they have persecuted me, they will also persecute you; if they have kept my saying, they will keep yours also.*

It is time for saints to become more and more like Jesus Christ. Although people will hate you, fight against you, and persecute you; You still must constantly increase in the likeness and image of Jesus Christ. You must talk like Jesus, live like Jesus, and work like Jesus. In all things people should be able to tell You have been with Jesus, and You are becoming more and more like Jesus each day.

> *(Acts.4:13) ¹³Now when they saw the boldness of Peter and John, and perceived that they were unlearned and ignorant men, they marvelled; and they took knowledge of them, that they had been with Jesus.*

> *(Galatians.4:19) ¹⁹My little children, of whom I travail in birth again until Christ be formed in you,*

I would rather be persecuted for being like Jesus than to be praised for being like the devil. The more you act like the devil, the less you will be persecuted. The more you live righteous in Christ Jesus, the more you will be persecuted.

(2nd Timothy.3:12-13) 12 Yea, and all that will live godly in Christ Jesus shall suffer persecution. 13 But evil men and seducers shall wax worse and worse, deceiving, and being deceived.

Father; I want to become so dedicated to You and Jesus Christ that I will count it a blessing to suffer shame for Your name sake.

(Acts.5:40-42) 40 And to him they agreed: and when they had called the apostles, and beaten them, they commanded that they should not speak in the name of Jesus, and let them go. 41 And they departed from the presence of the council, rejoicing that they were counted worthy to suffer shame for his name. 42 And daily in the temple, and in every house, they ceased not to teach and preach Jesus Christ.

Jesus my LORD; I must daily increase in being like You. I would rather be like You than to be like anyone else.

10. Israel will rebuild the temple and return to animal sacrifices

(Daniel 11:31) 31. And arms shall stand on his part, **<u>and they shall pollute the sanctuary of strength, and shall take away the daily sacrifice,</u>** *and they shall place the abomination that maketh desolate.*

(Revelation 11:1-2) 1. And there was given me a reed like unto a rod: and the angel stood, saying, **<u>Rise, and measure the temple of God</u>**, *and the altar, and them that worship therein. 2. But the court which is without the temple leave out, and measure it not; for it is given unto the Gentiles: and the holy city shall they tread under foot forty and two months.*

The Jewish temple will be rebuilt

In the last days, the nation of Israel will rebuild its temple on the original sight Solomon built it on. The problem with that is the Muslim's Dome of the Rock is now there. The Dome of the Rock is a key worship spot to all Muslims in which they will never willingly give up. Some believe the Jews will build their temple alongside the Dome. They believe that is why God tells John in *Revelation 11:2* not to measure the outer

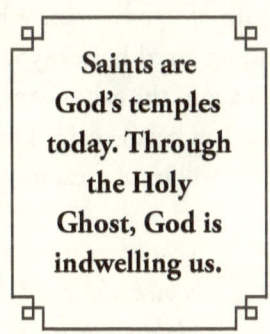

Saints are God's temples today. Through the Holy Ghost, God is indwelling us.

court. The outer court may be where the Dome of the Rock is. Others believe somehow the Jews will get the entire sight and destroy the Dome in order to rebuild the temple of God. While we are unsure which of these scenarios will happen, we are certain **the Jews will rebuild their temple**.

Animal sacrifices will start again

A key component of the worship service of the Jewish religion in the Old Testament was animal sacrifice. From the time the last Jewish temple was destroyed until this very day, it is believed that no constant animal sacrifices have been made. However, when the temple is rebuilt, the Old Testament ritual of animal sacrifices will be reinstated by the Jews. Daniel tells us that once the animal sacrifices begin, the Jews will make sacrifices daily. However, the antichrist will cause it to cease, and he will defile the temple.

> *(Daniel 9:27) 27. And he shall confirm the covenant with many for one week: and in the midst of the week **he shall cause the sacrifice and the oblation to cease**, and for the overspreading of abominations he shall make it desolate, even until the consummation, and that determined shall be poured upon the desolate.*

The ashes of the red heifer
(young red female cow)

While you may not totally understand what I am about to mention, it is something you need to know, and to watch for as we draw nearer to the return of Jesus Christ. When the Jewish religious leaders begin to talk about finding **a red heifer** (young female cow) without spot or blemish, or they talk about **the ashes of a red heifer**, realize it will not be long before animal sacrifices begin again. The sacrifice of the red heifer and the ashes of the red heifer will be of great importance in the ritual of the Jewish animal sacrifice.

> *(Numbers 19:2,5-6,9) 2. This is the ordinance of the law which the Lord hath commanded, saying, Speak unto the children of Israel, that they bring thee **a red heifer** without spot, wherein is no blemish, and upon which never came yoke: 5. **And one shall burn the heifer** in his sight; her skin, and her flesh, and her blood, with her dung, shall he burn: 6. And the priest shall take cedar wood, and hyssop, and scarlet, and cast it into the midst of the burning of the heifer. 9. And **a man that is clean shall gather up the ashes of the heifer**, and lay them up without the camp in a clean place, and it shall be kept for the congregation of the children of Israel for **a water of separation**: **it is a purification for sin**.*

The major reason the Jews will return to animal sacrifices is because they have rejected Jesus Christ as being the perfect sacrifice for their sins; and being their Messiah sent from God. They have rejected Him so much that many have become blind to the fact that He is the only Savior of the world and their only source of salvation.

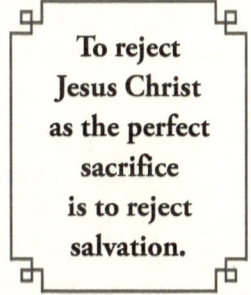

To reject Jesus Christ as the perfect sacrifice is to reject salvation.

During the Tribulation Period, the antichrist will cause so much torment, and tribulation to come upon the Jews that they will realize only Jesus can save them. They will realize Jesus is truly the Lord and Savior sent from God, and He is now the only One who can deliver them from the antichrist. They will also realize He is the only One who can save them from their sins. They will then call upon Him for salvation and deliverance. Jesus then will come and deliver them.

> (Romans 11:25-27) 25. For I would not, brethren, that ye should be ignorant of this mystery, lest ye should be wise in your own conceits; <u>**that blindness in part is happened to Israel, until the fulness of the Gentiles be come in**</u>. 26. And so <u>**all Israel shall be saved: as it is written, There shall come out of Sion the Deliverer**</u>, and shall turn away ungodliness from Jacob: 27. For this is my covenant unto them, when I shall take away their sins.

Even today many Jews are realizing that Jesus Christ is the true Messiah and is accepting Him as their Lord and Savior. The increasing number of Jews coming to Jesus shows we are in the last days. The blinders are coming off of them.

Only the true and living God
is a threat to the antichrist

The antichrist will not go into the Buddhist temple to defile it, nor will he go into the temple of Confucius to defile it. He will not be concerned about any other so-called gods because all others will be found to be false. The only real threat to him is **the true and living God whose name is called Jehovah, and His Son is Jesus Christ.** That is why he goes to the temple of God because he knows the God of the Jews (and Christians) is the **only** true and living God. Although He is the God of the Jews, a Jewish person will not become saved until he/she accepts Jesus Christ as Lord and Savior.

Father; the blood of animals and the blood of men could never take away sins and bring salvation. Only Your blood shed through your Son Jesus Christ can take away sins and bring salvation. Thank You for giving us Your blood by giving us Your Son. In Jesus' name I pray; amen.

Jesus my LORD; thank You for being the perfect sacrifice that made salvation available to all who will receive it. I rejoice that I have received it by receiving You.

11. The devil and the antichrist will make war against the saints of God

*(Revelation 12:17) 17. And the dragon was wroth with the woman, **and went to make war with the remnant of her seed, which keep the commandments of God, and have the testimony of Jesus Christ**. (Revelation 13:6-8) 6. And he opened his mouth in blasphemy against God, to blaspheme his name, and his tabernacle, and them that dwell in heaven. 7. **And it was given unto him to make war with the saints, and to overcome them**: and power was given him over all kindreds, and tongues, and nations. 8. And all that dwell upon the earth shall worship him, **whose names are not written in the book of life of the Lamb** slain from the foundation of the world.*

Just before and at the beginning of the Tribulation Period the world, the devil, and the antichrist will **persecute** saints. Eventually the world, the devil, and the antichrist will **declare all out war** against saints. The amazing thing about all of this is; even in the face of fierce, fiery, and ferocious fighting of the antichrist against saints, saints will refuse to fall down and worship him. They would rather die for Jesus than to live for the devil, serve the devil, or worship the devil.

In the last days, God will allow the devil, through the antichrist, to kill many of His saints (overcome them) to show him and the world that dying for Jesus is much better than living for the devil. God's saints will **love** Him so much they will willingly lay down their lives for Jesus Christ their Lord and Savior. God the Father will also grant them such powerful **grace** that dying for Jesus will be a wonderful and marvelous experience just as it was to Stephen.

*(Acts 7:54-60) 54. When they heard these things, they were cut to the heart, and they gnashed on him with their teeth. 55. But **he, being full of the Holy Ghost**, looked up stedfastly into heaven, and saw the glory of God, and Jesus standing on the right hand of God, 56. And said, Behold, I see the heavens*

opened, and the Son of man standing on the right hand of God. 57. Then they cried out with a loud voice, and stopped their ears, and ran upon him with one accord, 58. And cast him out of the city, **and stoned him***: and the witnesses laid down their clothes at a young man's feet, whose name was Saul. 59. And they stoned Stephen, calling upon God, and saying, Lord Jesus, receive my spirit. 60. And he kneeled down, and cried with a loud voice, Lord, lay not this sin to their charge.* ***And when he had said this, he fell asleep****.*

Never think just because the devil was able to kill a saint that the devil won. In actuality all the devil did was cause that saint to receive one of the greatest experiences of his life, and to receive tremendous eternal heavenly rewards. The greatest experience Stephen had occurred at his death. While we can not see it, the greatest experience many saints have in life happens at the time of their death; because at that time God opens heaven and shows them the glory of Himself, and the glorified Christ standing at His right hand.

Father; only by the anointing of Your Holy Spirit can a saint be faithful in the face of death. Thank You for anointing all who will face martyrdom to remain steadfast in You. In Jesus' name I pray; amen.

Jesus my LORD; I want to grow to the level where I love You more than I love life.

12. Many saints will be strong and do exploits

(Daniel.11:32) ³²And such as do wickedly against the covenant shall he corrupt by flatteries: **<u>but the people that do know their God shall be strong, and do exploits</u>**.

The servants of God who have grown in the knowledge of God will be strong, and by the power of the Holy Ghost will do exploits to the glory of God the Father in the name of the Lord Jesus Christ. They will see the sick healed, miracles being performed to the glory of Jesus Christ, and souls saved. They will be the devil's greatest threat, and regardless of what the devil does, they will continue living for Jesus, loving Jesus, and working for Jesus Christ.

(Ephesians.6:10) ¹⁰Finally, my brethren, be strong in the Lord, and in the power of his might.

To be strong in the Lord:

A. You must constantly grow in Your love for God. (John.14:15).

B. You must constantly grow in the knowledge of the Word. (2nd Peter.3:18).

C. You must constantly pray (Ephesians.6:18) and you must pray about everything. (Philippians.4:6).

D. You must have on, and keep on the whole armor of God (Ephesians.6:10-18).

E. You must worship God in spirit and in truth (John.4:24)

F. You must daily and constantly produce the fruit of the Spirit (Galatians,5:22-23).

G. You must be filled with the Holy Ghost (Acts.1:8).

H. You must be filled with the joy of the Lord (Nehemiah.8:10).

I. You must be filled with faith (Romans.4:20).

J. You must take up the weapons of your warfare. (2nd Corinthians.10:4-6).

K. You must flow in the gifts of the Spirit (1st Corinthians.12:1-11).

L. You must use the power of binding and loosing (Matthew.16:19).

M. Much, much more.

These are many of the things God has provided so saints can constantly increase in power, authority, and victory. All saints need to study these things and daily strive to implement them into their lives. Saints should also seek to constantly increase in these things so they can constantly increase in strength.

Father; I refuse to be a weak powerless servant of the Savior. You are too great a God for me to remain weak in You. I ask that You will help me and empower me to daily and constantly increase in my strength in You. In Jesus' name I pray; amen.

Jesus my LORD; because You want strong powerful servants, I purpose to daily increase in strength and power to Your glory by Your Spirit.

13. I have not told it all

While I have endeavored to reveal many of the things which will transpire among religions during the times of the end, I have not told it all. Many other interesting events will emerge and be revealed about the activities of religions and religious leaders as we advance closer and closer to the soon return of our wonderful Lord and Savior Jesus Christ.

I would strongly admonish you to embark upon an in-depth study on the subject of what religions will be doing in the last days. Ask God to lead you to the right material, teachers, and study guides which will increase your understanding of eschatology (the study of end time events).

> (2nd Timothy.2:15) [15] Study to show thyself approved unto God, a workman that needeth not to be ashamed, rightly dividing the word of truth.

Father; Your saints can not afford to be ignorant concerning what's about to happen during end times. Please continue moving in our lives to cause us to increase in the knowledge of end time events according to Your written Word. In Jesus' name I pray; amen.

> (Deuteronomy.29:29) [29] The secret things belong unto the LORD our God: but those things which are revealed belong unto us and to our children for ever, that we may do all the words of this law.

Jesus my LORD; I want to know all I can about Your soon return. Thank You for making that knowledge available for those who will seek it out through studying Your Holy written Word. Knowledge is power. The more I know about Your Word, the more powerful I become in You. I want to be as powerful in You as I can be.

> (Daniel.2:20-22) [20] Daniel answered and said, Blessed be the name of God for ever and ever: for wisdom and might are his: [21] And he changeth the times and the seasons: he removeth

kings, and setteth up kings: he giveth wisdom unto the wise, and knowledge to them that know understanding: ^{22}*He revealeth the deep and secret things: he knoweth what is in the darkness, and the light dwelleth with him.*

LESSON 12

What Nations Will Be Doing Just Before The Return of Jesus Christ Part. 1

What Nations Will Be Doing Just Before The Return of Jesus Christ

Topics of discussion

1. Keep an eye on all nations of the world.

2. Nations will fight against one another with advanced military weaponry.

With all the information God has made available concerning end time events; saints have no excuse for being ignorant concerning eschatology. With these things now unfolding in our world constantly, saints should be informed on what's going to happen next. While many events have been concealed until the time of the end; enough has been revealed for saints to know what nations are doing now, and what nations will do in the future.

Regardless of the things which may transpire concerning nations, saints must realize God is in control, and He has an eternal plan and purpose He is fulfilling. He will even allow the bases of men to rule, so His will can be done. Even when corruption fills the land and government; and chaos overflows in the streets, God knows, God sees, and God's plans will still be fulfilled concerning that land. What He prophesied will happen, will happen; regardless of the present condition of the people and nation.

> *(Daniel.4:17)* *¹⁷This matter is by the decree of the watchers, and the demand by the word of the holy ones: to the intent that the living may know that the most High ruleth in the kingdom of men, and giveth it to whomsoever he will, and setteth up over it the basest of men.*

1. Keep an eye on
all nations of the world

(Revelation 13:6-8) 6. And he opened his mouth in blasphemy against God, to blaspheme his name, and his tabernacle, and them that dwell in heaven. 7. And it was given unto him to make war with the saints, and to overcome them: ***and power was given him over all kindreds, and tongues, and nations***.

(Revelation 17:15) 15. And he saith unto me, The waters which thou sawest, where the whore sitteth, are peoples, and multitudes, **and nations**, *and tongues.*

One of the major keys of properly understanding Bible prophecy (**eschatology** = the study of end time events) is to notice what all nations of the world will be doing. End time prophecies are not isolated incidents which only deals with a few select nations. End time prophecies affect all nations of the earth.

> **Ask God to show you how nations today are lining up to fulfill Biblical prophecy. You will be surprised at what you see.**

Although many nations are not specifically named in the Holy Bible, all nations will be effected with the events of the last days. Therefore, all students of eschatology should become familiar with:

A. The nations of the world.

B. The nations mentioned in the Holy Bible which deals with end time events.

C. How each nation relates to and deals with the nation of Israel.

D. The geographical location of a nation from Israel (i.e. if the nation is north, east, or south of Israel).

E. The ancient names of nations. (See what a nation is called today, and then find out what that same nation was called in the days of the Old Testament and early New Testament.).

F. Things the Holy Bible says a nation will do. When You find a nation in our world doing it today, study and seek to find out if that is the nation the Bible was speaking of.

Ancient Biblical names:

When seeking to discover which nation or nations the Holy Bible is speaking of concerning Biblical prophecy, it is very important to look up its' ancient Biblical name. **When referring to nations; the Holy Bible does not use modern day names, unless that was the name of the nation in the days in which the Holy Bible was written.** Egypt is still called Egypt because that was its' ancient name. The name Israel is used because that was its' ancient name. When speaking of Russia the ancient names of *Gog, the land of Magog, the chief prince of Meshech and Tubal* are used. When speaking of Iraq and Iran the names of Arabia, Assyria, and Mede-Persia are used.

Geographical location:

Also notice the geographical locations of a nation. Nations north of Israel are sometimes called **the kings of the north**. Nations east of Israel are sometimes called **the kings of the east**. Nations south of Israel are sometimes called **the kings of the south**. Nations which were not mentioned in ancient Biblical times are included in the phrase **all nations**.

Review

A. The Holy Bible use ancient names of nations and kingdoms.

B. Learn what nation today now occupies the geographical area mentioned when an ancient name is used.

C. Learn the geographical location of a nation from Israel (north, south, or east).

D. Do not try to force a nation to fit into Bible prophecy. If it does not easily fit the prophecy, it's probably not the nation the Holy Bible is talking about.

E. A lot of what nations will be doing will be concealed until the time of the end.

> *(Daniel 12:4,9) 4. But thou, O Daniel,* **shut up the words, and seal the book, even to the time of the end**: *many shall run to and fro, and knowledge shall be increased. 9. And he said, Go thy way, Daniel:* **for the words are closed up and sealed till the time of the end**.

F. The geographical composition of this world is going to change so dramatically that it will be difficult at times to know which nation is being spoken of.

> *(Revelation 6:14) 14. And the heaven departed as a scroll when it is rolled together;* **and every mountain and island were moved out of their places**.

G. New nations will come forth in the last days which have not existed before.

> *(Revelation.17:21) 12. And the ten horns which thou sawest are ten kings,* **which have received no kingdom as yet**; *but receive power as kings one hour with the beast.*

H. Look at the events the Bible says will happen during the last days and then notice which nations are fulfilling these events.

Israel is the key
nation to watch

The nation of Israel is the key nation to watch when it comes to end time events. When the time comes that you see Jerusalem being surrounded by many armies of the world (coming to attack her), look up because Jesus Christ is soon to return.

> (Luke 21:20-22) 20. And **when ye shall see Jerusalem compassed with armies, then know that the desolation thereof is nigh.** 21. *Then let them which are in Judaea flee to the mountains; and let them which are in the midst of it depart out; and let not them that are in the countries enter thereinto. 22. For these be the days of vengeance,* **that all things which are written may be fulfilled**.

Key things to watch for
concerning nations

A. Israel becoming an independent nation again.

B. Constantly increasing hatred that many (and most) nations will have towards Israel.

C. The constant conflict between other nations and the nation of Israel.

D. The establishing of a seven-year peace treaty concerning Israel and nations around her during the Tribulation Period.

E. The rebuilding of the Jewish temple of God and the reinstitution of animal sacrifices.

F. The majority of Jews leaving all nations of the world and returning to Israel.

G. The development of a **ten nation confederacy** which will eventually be against Israel.

H. The resurgence of the Old Roman Empire governmental system.

I. Rebuilding of Babylon or Babylonian system.

J. Increase in military technology and weaponry which will allow men to take all life from the earth (Matthew.24:22).

K. An increasing interdependency of nations on one another economically.

L. Increasing talk of a one world ruling government or governmental counsel.

M. The development of a one world currency and economic system.

N. Institution of a cashless society where monetary transactions are done electronically.

O. The development of an international identification card or mark.

P. The failure of the economic system of many nations.

Q. A major increase in wars.

R. Increase in political unrest within nations which lead to internal conflicts, fighting, and wars.

S. More and more nations becoming antagonistic against Jesus Christ and those who serve Him.

T. The emergence of a charismatic world leader.

U. An increase in false miracle workers.

V. A push to unite all religions into one universal religion.

W. Developing technology which will enable nations to communicate with one another easily and/or instantly.

   1. Cell phones
   2. Internet
   3. Advance travel
   4. Instant international television through satellite linkups.

5. Computer technology which instantly translates languages from the language of the one speaking or typing; to the language of the one being spoken to.

X. Developing technology which allows those in authority to keep track of all products being bought or sold.

Y. The ability to implant microchips under or on the skin of animals and **people**.

Z. Increased robotic technology which will enable one to make an inanimate (lifeless) object appear to be living, speaking, and moving.

AA. Much, much.

One of the major reasons there is an explosion of knowledge in these last days and times is so men can perfect the technology needed to accomplish the things mentioned in Bible prophecy concerning end time events.

A. Having the ability to track all that is bought and sold.

B. Having the ability to make the image of the beast live and speak.

C. Having the ability to make it appear that one is calling fire down from heaven.

D. Having the ability to run to and fro over all the earth.

E. Having the ability to take all life from the earth.

F. Having the ability to gather all nations to battle in a place called Armageddon.

G. Etc.

Father; thank You for opening our eyes to end time events concerning nations, and concerning how modern technology fits into it. In Jesus' name I pray; amen.

Jesus my LORD; even so come quickly.

2. Nations will fight against one another with advanced military weaponry

*(Matthew 24:6-8) 6. **<u>And ye shall hear of wars and rumours of wars</u>**: see that ye be not troubled: for all these things must come to pass, but the end is not yet. 7. For **<u>nation shall rise against nation, and kingdom against kingdom</u>**: and there shall be famines, and pestilences, and earthquakes, in divers places. 8. All these are the beginning of sorrows.*

*(Mark 13:7-8) 7. And when ye shall hear of wars and rumours of wars, be ye not troubled: for such things must needs be; but the end shall not be yet. 8. **<u>For nation shall rise against nation, and kingdom against kingdom</u>**: and there shall be earthquakes in divers places, and there shall be famines and troubles: these are the beginnings of sorrows.*

One of the mistakes people make is to take one facet of Biblical prophecy and not connect it with other parts of Biblical prophecies. When World War I, and World War II were happening, many preached the world was about to end because of the wars and rumors of wars. They fail to realize these wars were only **the beginning of sorrows,** and there were yet other Bible prophecies that had to come to pass along with wars and rumors of wars. The major prophecy not fulfilled during the times of World War I & II was the prophecy of Israel becoming a mighty nation again and the things which would happen to her.

In order to have an accurate view of prophecy you must endeavor to place **all** prophetic events together in their proper order and in their proper time sequence.

Just before the Tribulation Period, and at the beginning of the Tribulation Period, there will be so many military conflicts going on that the antichrist will rise to great popularity and power by promising to bring peace to the world. His ultimate goals however will be, (1) to rule the world, (2) to kill as many people as he can, (3) to eventually destroy the world and (4) take as many to hell with him as he can.

Before the antichrist come promising peace, safety, and prosperity; men will have developed such powerful weapons of destruction that they will have the ability to take all life from the earth (Matthew.24:22). Because of these massive weapons of destruction many will seek for someone to bring peace among men before men totally destroy themselves. Instead of seeking God through His Son Jesus Christ to bring peace, they will turn to the antichrist.

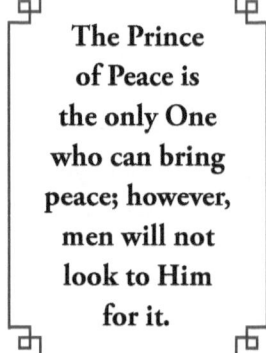

The Prince of Peace is the only One who can bring peace; however, men will not look to Him for it.

I believe men will eventually use nuclear weapons against one another. The Holy Bible discusses and describes the effects a nuclear weapon has, (1) upon a person, (2) upon a nation, and (3) upon the world. Listed below is a description of what **I believe** the Holy Bible says about nuclear weapons.

Nuclear weapons

A. **The Holy Bible calls nuclear weapons the ability to take all life (all flesh) from the earth** *(Matthew 24:22) 22. And except those days should be shortened,* **there should no flesh be saved***: but for the elect's sake those days shall be shortened.*

> Until the development of nuclear weapons, it was inconceivable that men could do anything which would cause the total elimination of all flesh from the earth. Once nuclear weapons were developed and men saw the destruction and devastation they could cause, men realized they had developed something that could totally wipe out all of earth's population. All human life, animal life, insect life and all vegetation life can now be eliminated as a direct result of nuclear war, nuclear winter, and nuclear fallout.

B. **The Holy Bible suggests that nuclear weapons will be used in wars to help kill 1/4 of the earth's population.** *(Revelation 6:7-8) 7. And when he had opened the fourth seal, I heard the voice of the fourth beast say, Come and see. 8. And I looked, and behold a pale horse: and his name that sat on him was Death, and Hell followed with him. And power was given unto them <u>**over the fourth part of the earth**</u>, <u>**to kill with sword**</u>, and with hunger, and with death, and with the beasts of the earth.*

Many believe that the part of this scripture which says "**to kill with sword**" is referencing to the use of nuclear weapons. In *Revelation 6:4* it tells of a **great sword** (a great weapon of war) which was given to them to make wars.

*(Revelation 6:4) 4. And there went out another horse that was red: and power was given to him that sat thereon to take peace from the earth, and that they should kill one another: <u>**and there was given unto him a great sword**</u>.*

As we watch the news today, we notice an increase in nations seeking to acquire nuclear weapons. Radical nations aimed at destroying Israel and America are striving with all that is within them to gain such weaponry.

C. **Zechariah describes the effects that nuclear weapons have upon the human body.** *(Zechariah 14:12) 12. And this shall be the plague wherewith the Lord will smite all the people that have fought against Jerusalem; <u>**Their flesh**</u> shall consume away <u>**while they stand upon their feet**</u>, and <u>**their eyes shall consume away**</u> in their holes, and <u>**their tongue shall consume away in their mouth**</u>.*

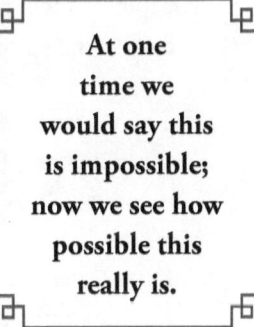

At one time we would say this is impossible; now we see how possible this really is.

This describes exactly what happens to someone in the midst of a nuclear explosion. **Their eyes** melt away in their sockets; **their tongue** melts away in their mouth, and **their flesh** burns off their bones. All these things happen while the person is still standing upon their feet. The heat is so intense that before their dead bodies can fall to the ground all their flesh is consumed and melted away.

D. **The nuclear weapon which will destroy the city of Babylon is discussed in the Bible.** *(Revelation 18:8,18-19,21) 8. Therefore shall her plagues come in one day, death, and mourning, and famine; and she shall be **utterly burned with fire**: for strong is the Lord God who judgeth her. 18. And cried when they saw **the smoke of her burning**, saying, What city is like unto this great city! 19. And they cast dust on their heads, and cried, weeping and wailing, saying, Alas, alas, that great city, wherein were made rich all that had ships in the sea by reason of her costliness! **for in one hour is she made desolate**. 21. And a mighty angel took up **a stone like a great millstone**, and cast it into the sea, saying, Thus **with violence** shall that great city Babylon be thrown down, **and shall be found no more at all**.*

1. Only a nuclear explosion can destroy, in one hour, a city the size that the rebuilt New Babylon will be. *(Revelation 18:17,19)*.

2. Only a nuclear explosion can totally destroy a city in such a way that no one could find any part of the city. *(Revelation 18:21)*.

3. The smoke from the mushroom cloud produced from a nuclear explosion will rise for miles and can be seen from far away. The Bible calls it the smoke of her burning *(Revelation 18:18)*.

4. The violence of the explosion described in Revelation 18 represents the violence of a nuclear explosion. It is described as a millstone being cast into the sea. *(Revelation 18:21)*.

5. If you were to take a millstone and cast it into the sea, the end results would resemble a nuclear explosion. As the stone hits the water, water will jump up and then fall back down. The waves will then spread throughout the water. During a nuclear explosion, a mushroom cloud will rise up, and then smoke, fire, and nuclear fallout will spread outward for miles.

E. **The armies which will use nuclear weapons are described.** *(Joel 2:3-6)*
3. A fire devoureth before them; and behind them a flame burneth: the land is as the garden of Eden before them, and behind them a desolate wilderness; yea, and nothing shall escape them. 4. The appearance of them is as the appearance of horses; and as horsemen, so shall they run. 5. Like the noise of chariots on the tops of mountains shall they leap, like the noise of a flame of fire that devoureth the stubble, as a strong people set in battle array. 6. Before their face the people shall be much pained: all faces shall gather blackness.

1. I believe this army will use conventional weapons on a land when they first enter into it. Then after spoiling the land they will use nuclear weapons to totally annihilate and desecrate the land. Before they enter the land, the land will look as beautiful as the Garden of Eden; however, when they are finished with the land, the land will be a barren desolate wilderness because they will devastate it with nuclear weapons.

> **Now you understand why so many nations are seeking to acquire nuclear weapons**

2. This army will have on bulletproof armor (body armor); thus when they are shot, they will not fall but keep marching and destroying. *(Joel 2:8)* 8. *Neither shall one thrust another; they shall walk every one in his path: and **when they fall upon the sword, they shall not be wounded**.*

New kinds of weapons, new war machines, and new kinds of soldiers will be developed

When the prophets of the Old and New Testament wrote their prophecies they had no idea of the kinds of military technology that would eventually be developed in these modern times in which we now live. All they had during those times were swords, knives, spears, shields, chariots, horses, and other equipment that we today would call ancient medieval weaponry. That is why they used terms like horses, swords, shields, chariots, bows, and arrows, etc. when addressing prophetic events of today.

The prophets of old could not in their wildest dreams conceive of such things as jet planes, automobiles, satellite technology, television, cell phones, laser guided missiles, nuclear weapons, germ-warfare, weapons of mass destruction, and many of the other technological advancements of today and tomorrow. Also, remember that these type weapons would not be invented until thousands of years after the writings of the prophets. Those who would read the prophecies before these types of modern day weapons were invented could only understand the terms the prophets used. However, we today who read their prophecies know how modern day weapons fit perfectly into their prophecies. That is why we can translate the words "**a great sword**" into "**a great weapon of war**", or "**a great weapon of mass destruction**".

As time progresses and if God delays Jesus' coming, men will develop new weapons of war, and new war machines that we today could not imagine. Technology is advancing at such a rapid pace it is hard to imagine what new weapons of war men will eventually develop.

With the experimentation today of robotics and artificial intelligence, it would not be surprising if men developed new soldiers in the form of robots, or in the form of robotic machinery connected to human bodies. Mechanical men and machines may be developed in such ways that guns, bombs, and chemical weapons will have little to no effect on them. The cold of winter, the rains of spring, and the heat of summer will not affect them. They will be strong, fast, and invincible. It will not be surprising to me the things the mind of men will be able to develop in the last days.

Saints of God need to count themselves blessed for being able to live in a time when Bible prophecies are being fulfilled at such an alarming rate. To read what the prophets wrote, and then see them unfolding in our world today is exciting.

Seeing these things manifesting should cause saints to live holy, serve God with all our hearts, and extend an invitation to salvation to sinners as often as we can. We should pray for souls to be saved, worship Jesus for providing salvation, and seek to prepare people for the events of these last days. Saints should realize Jesus is coming soon; thus we need to be about our Father's business.

Father; You said this would happen; now it's happening. Thank You for allowing me to be born in such exciting times as this. Please use me and all saints according to Your will during these end times. In Jesus' name I pray; amen.

Jesus my LORD; You birth me into this world in this season for a Divine reason. Lord, by the power of the Holy Ghost, I truly want to fulfill that reason.

What Nations Will Be Doing Just Before The Return of Jesus Christ Part. 2

What nations will be doing Pt. 2

Topics of discussion

3. Israel will become a mighty nation again and will eventually be hated by the entire world.

4. Babylon will be rebuilt.

5. New kings and kingdoms shooting forth.

6. Nations will seek to form a one-world government with a one world economic system.

7. The Holy Bible is the only book of accurate prophecy.

What are you doing for Jesus Christ in these end times? Are you praying for souls to be saved? Are you witnessing to sinners? Are you living righteous? Are you being a light for the glory of God? Just what are You doing in these end times?

Father; the time is late, and the day is far spent. Please anoint saints to redeem the time, and make full proof of our lives, ministry, and possessions. In Jesus' name I pray; amen.

Jesus my LORD; I want You to use me to the fullest of Your will in these last days. I don't have time to waste nor opportunities to squander. I must take full advantage of all You made available to saints so we can be mightily used of You in these last days. Lord; here am I; use me.

3. Israel will become a mighty nation again and will eventually be hated by the entire world

*(Matthew 24:32-34) 32. Now learn a parable of **the fig tree**; When his branch is yet tender, and putteth forth leaves, ye know that summer is nigh: 33. So likewise ye, when ye shall see all these things, know that it is near, even at the doors. 34. Verily I say unto you, **This generation shall not pass, till all these things be fulfilled***

A. In the last days Israel will become a blessed nation. It will become a wealthy nation and a mighty nation militarily. (*Matthew 24:32-33, Micah.4:1*).

B. Israel will be hated of her neighbors (*Zechariah 12:2*) and will be in constant conflict with them.

C. Israel will eventually be hated by all nations (*Zechariah 14:2,9*). All nations will come to battle against Israel (*Zechariah 12:2,*) but God will deliver her.

D. Israel will rebuild her temple and return to animal sacrifices. (*Daniel 9:27, Revelation 11:1-2*).

E. Israel will sign a peace treaty with the antichrist. **This will start the Tribulation Period.** It will be for seven years but the antichrist will break it within 3 ½ years. (*Daniel 9:27*).

F. Russia and certain nations will come to fight against Israel (*Ezekiel 38:14-16*) but God will protect her and deliver her.

G. The antichrist will defile her temple. (*2nd Thessalonians 2:4-5*).

H. The devil will seek to persecute the Jews once he is no longer allowed to enter into heaven, however, the Jews will flee into the wilderness where

God has prepared a place for her for times, times, and ½ a time (2 ½ years). (*Revelation 12:7-14*).

I. As the Jews flee into the wilderness, the devil will cause a flood of people to come against the Jews, however, the earth will open up as it did in the days of Moses (*Numbers 16:28-35*) and swallow them (*Revelation 12:14-17*), then the devil will seek to persecute saints.

J. Jerusalem will then become such a wicked city during this time of the Tribulation Period that God will refer to her as **<u>spiritual Sodom and Egypt</u>** (*Revelation 11:8*).

K. **Two powerful witnesses** who possessed the same anointing as Moses and Elijah will prophesy for 3½ years in Jerusalem while working miracles, signs and wonders. However, at the end of their prophecy they shall be killed by the beast which came up out of the bottomless pit. Their dead bodies will lie in the streets of Jerusalem for 3½ days and then they will arise from the dead and ascend up into heaven. (*Revelation 11: 3-12*).

L. After the two witnesses ascend into heaven, there will be a great earthquake in Jerusalem in which 1/10th part of the city will be destroyed, and seven thousand people will die. (*Revelation 11:13*).

M. At the end of the Millennium (1000-year reign of Christ and His saints) the devil will cause Gog and Magog to come against the beloved city Jerusalem, but God will send fire down from heaven and destroy them. (*Revelation 20:7-9*).

N. In Eternity Future, there will be a **New Jerusalem** which comes down from heaven adorned as a bride prepared for her husband. (*Revelation 21:10-27*).

There will be many, many more things happening to Israel during the last days that we have not mentioned. Through personal study on your own, you will learn what these things are, and when they will happen.

4. Babylon will be rebuilt

(Revelation 18:1-4) 1. And after these things I saw another angel come down from heaven, having great power; and the earth was lightened with his glory. 2. And he cried mightily with a strong voice, saying, **Babylon the great** *is fallen, is fallen, and is become the habitation of devils, and the hold of every foul spirit, and a cage of every unclean and hateful bird. 3. For all nations have drunk of the wine of the wrath of her fornication, and the kings of the earth have committed fornication with her, and the merchants of the earth are waxed rich through the abundance of her delicacies. 4. And I heard another voice from heaven, saying, Come out of her, my people, that ye be not partakers of her sins, and that ye receive not of her plagues.*

Because we are endeavoring to keep this study short and simple, we will only mention the attributes of this new rebuilt city without making comments on them. As you study the scriptures we give, and as you study the writing of other notable eschatology theologians you will learn more and more about Babylon. You will also learn more and more about how there will be a great transfer of wealth to that region of the world.

It is unclear if this is referring to the actual ancient city of Babylon being rebuilt, or if it is referring to a governmental system that resembles the ancient city of Babylon. It may even refer to a modern day city that has the attributes of the ancient city of Babylon.

A. It will become a great city (*Revelation 16:19;18:16*).

B. It will become a city of wealth (*Revelation 18:11-16*).

C. It will be a city given over into the hands of demons, foul spirits, and unclean and hateful birds (extremely wicked demonic spirits) (*Revelation 18:2-3*), and unto sorcery (*Revelation 18:23*).

D. It will become a great city of wickedness (*Revelation 17:5, 18:1-5*).

E. It will be a city where many of the saints of God will live and work (Revelation.18:4).

F. It will become a city totally against the saints of Jesus Christ. The people of the city of Babylon will eventually begin to persecute, imprison, and kill saints of God. (*Revelation 17:6, 18:24*).

G. It will be a city that God will judge *(Revelation. 14:7-8) (Revelation. 18:1-8)*

H. It will be destroyed by a nuclear explosion (*Revelation 18:16-22*).

Some try to equate the scriptures referring to Babylon of the last days as being one of the existing cities or nations of today. Some say it's America or some other powerful nation or city of today. They give many reasons why they hold to this theory, and they seek to reinforce their belief with scriptural references. I would admonish you to do an in-depth study for yourself to confirm or dispute this belief.

Father; thank You for revealing unto us things which will happen in the last days. In Jesus' name I pray; amen.

Jesus my LORD; I do not want to live in a city as wicked as Babylon will become. However, if I do, please empower me to be a light of righteousness to Your glory.

5. New kings and kingdoms shooting forth

As you read the book of Daniel, Revelation, and other books of the Holy Bible you will notice **during the time of the Tribulation Period** many new kings and kingdoms will shoot forth.

> *(Revelation 17:12-13)* 12. **<u>And the ten horns which thou sawest are ten kings, which have received no kingdom as yet; but receive power as kings one hour with the beast</u>**. 3. *These have one mind, and shall give their power and strength unto the beast.*

<u>To receive power one-hour means; for a relatively short period of time.</u>

Things are about to drastically change in our world and in the political composition of nations. A great transfer of wealth and power is about to occur, and kingdoms never heard of before will emerge with power, might, and great loyalty to the antichrist.

Many nations which were once considered to be insignificant and third world countries will rise to prominence as major players on the world stage. Also, islands, mountains, and landmasses will be changed dramatically because of earthquakes and other national catastrophes.

When it comes to Bible prophecy we are living in exciting times. That which the prophets have prophesied about, we now see happening in our lives today. **However, what we have seen does not compare to the things we are about to see.** Do not allow the things you are about to see trouble you because God is still in overall control. He is also in control of you and your life if you have accepted Jesus Christ as your Lord and Savior.

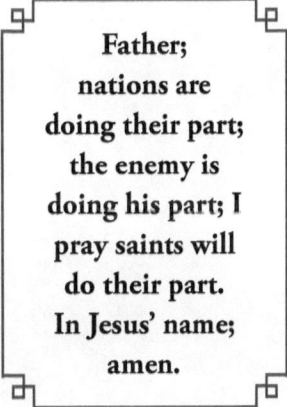

Father; nations are doing their part; the enemy is doing his part; I pray saints will do their part. In Jesus' name; amen.

When studying eschatology, it is important to study what has happened in the past, notice what is happening now, and learn what is going to happen in the future as revealed in the written Word of God. While we may not know who these new kings and kingdoms are, we do know they will emerge in the last days.

Father; You know the end from the beginning. Before something starts up; You know how it will end up. You are the omniscient (all-wise, all-seeing, all-knowing) God. If nations do good or if they do evil; You will be glorified through them; and they will not alter Your eternal plan for mankind. Thank You Father for being powerful enough to bring Your eternal purposes to full manifestation. In Jesus' name I pray; amen.

Jesus my LORD; thank You for making me, and all saints, a part of Your eternal plan for good, blessing, and salvation. I love You my Lord, Savior and Redeemer.

6. Nations will seek to form a one-world government with a one world economic system

*(Revelation 13:7-9) 7. And it was given unto him to make war with the saints, and to overcome them: and **power was given him over all kindreds, and tongues, and nations**.*

Many of our political leaders are constantly talking about a new world order in which all nations will be able to come together under one banner. Many things are being established to help this one world government come into existence. Some of the things happening are:

A. Nations coming together militarily under the banner of the United Nations and/or other organizations such as NATO, the League of Nations, European Common Market, etc.

B. Worldwide merging of economic systems because many nations are becoming dependent upon one another financially through trade and businesses. Some nations are failing economically, and because of the collapse of their economy, they will need help from other nations.

> **I do not look forward to the coming of the antichrist and his temporary kingdom; I look forward to the coming of Jesus Christ and His Eternal Kingdom where He is King, Ruler, and God.**

C. A worldwide electronic banking system. I believe that all financial transactions will be done electronically and that eventually paper and coin transactions will be done away with.

D. Global marketing system through the internet and through other electronic means.

E. Development of national and international identification cards, badges, and/or a computer chips implanted in or on ones' body somewhere (most likely on the forehead or right hand).

F. The disorder and chaos caused by the Rapture of the church.

G. The promise of the antichrist to bring unity, harmony, and stability back to the world after the Rapture of the church (if the church is raptured before the Tribulation Period).

Father; modern technology is being used to cause Biblical prophecies to come to pass. Although the prophets did not know what was going to be invented in the last days, these inventions precipitates, hasten, and greatly accelerates the manifestation of end time events. Thank You for being in overall control of end time events. In Jesus' name I pray; amen.

Jesus my LORD; I look forward to the time when Your Eternal Kingdom will be set up on earth. I gladly and willingly call You King, Ruler, and Potentate.

7. The Holy Bible is the only book of accurate prophecy

(Isaiah.42:9) 9. Behold, the former things are come to pass, and new things do I declare: before they spring forth I tell you of them

(Isaiah.46:9-10) ⁹Remember the former things of old: for I am God, and there is none else; I am God, and there is none like me, ¹⁰Declaring the end from the beginning, and from ancient times the things that are not yet done, saying, My counsel shall stand, and I will do all my pleasure:

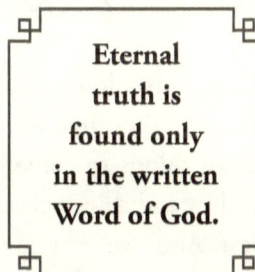

Eternal truth is found only in the written Word of God.

We are living in the time when we can read the prophecies of the Holy Bible, and then look around at our world and actually see them being fulfilled. They are being fulfilled just as they were given and in the order and manner the Holy Bible says they will occur.

(Matthew.24:33-34) ³³So likewise ye, when ye shall see all these things, know that it is near, even at the doors. ³⁴Verily I say unto you, This generation shall not pass, till all these things be fulfilled.

Always remember I am not telling it all. There are many more things which will transpire among nations and within nations during these last days that I have not mentioned. The study of end time events (eschatology) should be a continuing study of yours where you constantly learn new and exciting things.

Also certain things which will happen will not be reveal to saints until we come closer and closer to the end.

(Daniel.12:4, 9) ⁴But thou, O Daniel, shut up the words, and seal the book, even to the time of the end: many shall run to

and fro, and knowledge shall be increased. ⁹And he said, Go thy way, Daniel: for the words are closed up and sealed till the time of the end

(Revelation.10:4) ⁴And when the seven thunders had uttered their voices, I was about to write: and I heard a voice from heaven saying unto me, Seal up those things which the seven thunders uttered, and write them not.

As we draw closer and closer to the coming of Jesus Christ, the Holy Spirit will give illumination, enlightenment, and revelation knowledge to saints about things to come. Saints will be able to see things, know things, and understand things about end time events that was hidden from them in the past. Also, we have the Holy Spirit living in us to enlighten our hearts and minds concerning end time events. *(John.16:13-14) ¹³Howbeit when he, the Spirit of truth, is come, he will guide you into all truth: for he shall not speak of himself; but whatsoever he shall hear, that shall he speak: and he will show you things to come. ¹⁴He shall glorify me: for he shall receive of mine, and shall show it unto you.*

Father; thank You for the things You have revealed concerning end time prophecies. Please help saints to govern themselves according to Your Word and will. In Jesus' name I pray; amen.

Jesus my LORD. Your will, Your way, in Your timing.

The Great Tribulation Period

Some believe it will last 7years
Revelation.6-19

The Tribulation Period

Eventually many nations of the world will declare war against Israel, and make preparations to come against her to battle. However; a great charismatic world leader will propose an acceptable seven-year peace treaty between Israel and her enemies. That charismatic leader will be the antichrist; however; many will not realize it. When Israel and her enemies sign the seven-year peace treaty, the Tribulation Period will begin. After three and one half years, the antichrist will break the treaty, defile the temple, and then sit in the temple proclaiming himself to be God. Therefore, the last 3½ years, will be called **"The Great Tribulation Period."**

> *(Matthew.24:21-22) 21. For then shall be **great tribulation**, such as was not since the beginning of the world to this time, no, nor ever shall be. 22. And except those days should be shortened, there should no flesh be saved: but for the elect's sake those days shall be shortened.*

Events that will happen during The Tribulation Period

The seven seals
(Revelation.6:1-17, 7:1-17, 8:1-6)

1st seal; the white horse of religious deception (Revelation.6:1-2 Matthew.24:5) Religious deception will fill the world. The major goal of deceptive religious leaders will be to unite all religion into a one worldwide religion. The rider of this white horse is not Jesus because Jesus has many crowns while this rider has only one crown. Jesus has a sword; this rider has a bow. This rider is trying to imitate Jesus; thus he is false religion coming to deceive many.

2nd seal; the red horse of war (Revelation.6:3-4 Matthew.24:6-7) There will be wars and rumors of wars. According to Revelation.2:4 all nations will be involved in wars because the rider of this red horse **will take peace from the earth**. I believe that nuclear weapons will be used during some of these military conflicts.

3rd seal; the black horse of famine (Revelation.6:5-6 Matthew.24:7) There will be great famine in the land. A famine is a massive shortage of food, water, and many of the staples of life. As a result of the greed of man, wars, and natural disasters; there will be a massive shortage of food, clean water, clothing, shelter and other staples of life.

4th seal; the pale horse of pestilence (Revelation.6:7-8 Matthew.24:7) Great pestilences will be in the world. A pestilence is anything which kills on a massive level. During this time ¼ of earth's population will die. Even today sickness is on an increase, and many of the medicines used to treat certain sickness cause greater side effects than the sickness itself. People will die from diseases at a faster and higher rate than any other time in human history.

5th seal; the persecution of saints (Revelation.6:9-11 Matthew.24:9) There will be great persecution of and killing of saints. Souls of martyred saints will be under the altar of God waiting for God to bring judgment upon those who have killed them. As we draw closer to the soon return of Jesus Christ, the hatred of saints by the world will greatly increase.

6th seal; great and mighty catastrophes in the physical creation (Revelation.6:12,14 Matthew.24:7) There will be great earthquakes. One earthquake will be so bad that every mountain and island will be moved out of there place. The geographical composition of the earth will be totally changed.

The powers of heaven shall be shaken. (Revelation.6:12-17 Luke.21:25-26). The sun will refuse to shine, the moon will become as blood, and the stars shall fall from heaven.

Men's hearts will fail them for fear, (Revelation.6:15-17 Luke.21:26) and for looking after those things which are coming on the earth. Fearful sights will engulf men and leave them devastated and distressed.

Men will hide in caves asking the rocks to fall on them (Revelation.6:15-17) to hide them from Him that sits on the throne and from the wrath of the Lamb. They will realize that the great day of His wrath has come.

144,000 of God's Jewish servants are sealed with the seal of God. (Revelation.7:1-4) 12,000 from each of the 12 tribes of the children of Israel will be sealed. It is not revealed what this seal is, or if it will be visible for sinners to see. This seal will protect them from demons and from many of the natural disasters that will happen during this time. This seal will empower them to mightily witness to sinners and serve God during this evil time period.

The martyred Tribulation saints before the throne of God praising Him. (Revelation.7:9-17) There will be many saints killed for the cause of Christ during the Tribulation Period. God's grace will be upon them so powerfully that they will count it a glorious privilege to die for Jesus. Also they will receive great and awesome rewards in heaven.

7th seal. Preparing for the 7 trumpets. (Revelation.8:6). When this seal is opened there will be silence in heaven for half an hour; then seven angels will come forth with seven trumpets and will prepare to sound them.

The seven Trumpets

(Revelation.8-9)

1st trumpet. (Revelation.8:7) Hail and fire mixed with blood falls upon the earth. 1/3 of all trees, and all green grass will be burned up.

2nd trumpet. (Revelation.8:8) A great mountain (meteor) burning with fire falls from heaven into the sea causing 1/3 of the seas to turn to blood, 1/3 of fish dies, and 1/3 of all ships destroyed.

3rd trumpet. (Revelation.8:9-11) The star Wormwood falls from heaven into 1/3 of rivers and streams causing drinking water to become poisoned. Many men died from drinking the water.

4th trumpet. (Revelation.8:12) The sun, moon, and stars are smitten so that they will not shine for 1/3 of the time. 1/3 of the day the sun will not shine.

(Revelation. 8:13) An angel flies through heaven saying "**Woe, woe, woe**".

The 1st Woe

5th trumpet. (Revelation.9:1-12) A demon (called a star) falls from heaven with the key to the bottomless pit. He opens it and smoke comes out. From the smoke demons which look like locust come out to torment men with great pain for 5 months. The pain will be so great men will try to die but will not be able to die, because death will flee from them. These demons that look like locusts will have a king over them call Aboddon in Hebrew, and Apollyon in Greek.

The 2nd Woe

6th trumpet. (Revelation.9:13-21) The four angels (demons) bound in the great river Euphrates are loosed. They kill 1/3 of earth's population. **(The saints of God are not harmed or killed by any of these trumpet**

judgments). Although all of this will be going on, sinful men still will not repent of worshiping demons, committing murder, fornication, and stealing (Revelation.9:20-21).

7th thunders will utter their voice; however, the prophet John was not allowed to write down what they said (Revelation.10:1-7). It will not be known what they said until it actually happens during the Tribulation Period.

A little book: John was given a little book to eat which was sweet as honey in his mouth, but it made his belly bitter (Revelation.10:8-11). I believe this symbolized that John was to receive the Word of God in His heart; then give it out to many, many people. He is now doing that through the Book of Revelation which God had him to write.

The measuring of the temple but the outer court is not to be measured (Revelation.11:1-2). The outer court is given to the gentiles. It is believed that today the dome of the rock is built on the sight were the outer court of the temple is.

(Revelation.11:1-2, 2nd Thessalonians.2:4). The antichrist will eventually break the peace treaty he made with Israel at the beginning of the Tribulation Period. He will seek to destroy the Jews and will defile their temple by going into the temple, **sitting in it declaring he is God** (this is called the abomination of desolation spoken of by Daniel the prophet). This will happen at the mid-point of the Tribulation Period and there will be 42 months left (Revelation.11:2)

God's two witnesses: (Revelation.11:3-14) God's two witnesses will prophesy 1260 days (42 months) clothed in sackcloth. Fire comes out of their mouth to destroy their enemies, and they will shut up heaven that it rain not in the days of their prophecy. They can turn water into blood, and can smite the earth with all kinds of plagues. After they have finished their work of service for God, the beast that ascended out of the bottomless pit shall make war against them and shall kill them. Their dead bodies will lay in the streets of Jerusalem for three and one half days while all the earth rejoices over their death. After three days and a half they will rise from the dead and ascend up into heaven. Then there will be a great earthquake which shall kill 7000 people.

The 3rd Woe

7th trumpet (Revelation11:15-19) Great voices from heaven proclaim that the kingdoms of this world are become the kingdom of our Lord and His Christ. And on earth there were lightnings, and voices, and thunderings, and an earthquake, and great hail. It is surprising how sinners can remain sinners at this time. Hearing the voices speaking from heaven should cause all sinners to want to become saved; but they will not become saved.

satan (the great red dragon) will be kicked out of heaven: (Revelation.12:1-12) satan (the great red dragon) will be kicked out of heaven by Michael the archangel. satan will draw 1/3 of the angels down with him. he will try to destroy the Jews (as they flee from Jerusalem) by sending a great flood of people after them but the earth shall open up and swallow them. The devil will then persecute the saints of Jesus Christ.

The antichrist kingdom: (Revelation.13:1-10) The antichrist kingdom will come to its' fullness. The antichrist will rule all the world. he is the beast that comes up out of the sea having seven heads and ten horns. The antichrist is often called "**the beast**" in scripture.

The false prophet (Revelation.13:11-18) The false prophet sets up his kingdom. he is the beast which comes out of the earth with two horns like a lamb. he will work great miracles, and he will make an image of the beast and then cause all men to worship the beast and the image of the beast. he causes the image of the beast to speak. This false prophet will try to cause everyone to get **the mark of the beast,** or the **name of the beast**, or **the number of His name which is (666),** in their forehead or hand. Without one of those three things on them, they will not be able to buy or sale anything. The people of God will not get the mark.

The Lamb standing on Mount Sion (Revelation.14:1-5) with Him are 144,000 saints.

The seven angels
Of Revelation 14
(Revelation.14:6-20)

1st Angel (Revelation.14:6-7) an angel will fly through the sky preaching the everlasting gospel.

2nd Angel (Revelation.14:8) an angel cries out saying, "Babylon is fallen, is fallen . . ."

3rd Angel (Revelation.14:9-13) an angel cries out saying "If any man worship the beast and his image, and receive his mark in his forehead, or in his hand, The same shall drink of the wine of the wrath of God, poured out without mixture.

4th Angel (Revelation.14:14) the appearing of an angel like the Son of man having on his head a golden crown and in his hand a sharp sickle. (Some think this is Jesus Christ, but I do not think so because Jesus Christ has many crowns, and He has a sword and not a sickle)

5th Angel (Revelation.14:15) an angel cries out to the 4th angel saying, "Thrust in thy sickle, and reap: for the time is come for thee to reap; for the harvest of the earth is ripe." The 4th angel cast his sickle in the earth and the earth was reaped.

6th Angel (Revelation.14:17) another angel comes out of the temple which is in heaven. He also had a sharp sickle.

7th Angel (Revelation.14:18-20) another angel comes from the altar and cried with a loud voice to the 6th angel saying, "Thrust in thy sharp sickle, and gather the clusters of the vine of the earth; for her grapes are fully ripe." The 6th angel thrust his sickle into the earth.

The seven angels with the seven vials of the wrath of God.

Seven angels with seven last plagues (Revelation.15-16)

1st Vial (Revelation.16:2) Noisome and grievous sores on men

2nd Vial (Revelation.16:3) The sea become as the blood of a dead man

3rd Vial (Revelation.16:4-7) Rivers and fountains of **water become blood**

4th Vial (Revelation.16:8-9) Men scorched with fire and **great heat**

5th Vial (Rev.16:10-11) The kingdom of the beast becomes **dark and full of great pain**

6th Vial (Revelation.16:12-16) The River Euphrates is dried up to prepare a way for the kings of the east. **Three unclean spirits like frogs** come out of the mouth of the dragon (the devil), the beast (the antichrist), and the false prophet (the antichrist's helper). These are devils working miracles to gather men for the battle of the great day of God Almighty at a place called **Armageddon**.

7th Vial (Revelation.16:17-21) A great voice from heaven speaks saying, "It is done". There were voices, thunder, and lightening. There was a great earthquake that was the worst this world has ever seen. The great city was divided into three parts, the nations of the earth fall, every island fled away, and the mountains were not found. And there fail great hail from heaven each whose weight was about a talent. Men blasphemed God because the pain of the plague was great.

MYSTERY, BABYLON THE GREAT, THE MOTHER OF HARLOTS AND ABOMINATIONS OF THE EARTH
(Revelation.17)

1. This is a great false religious and political leader **and her kingdom** attempting to form a one world religion. This leader and this one world religion will be destroyed.

2. She committed spiritual fornication with the kings of this world (she causes them to worship false gods, the devil, and demons).

3. She was drunk with the blood of the saints and martyrs of Jesus Christ (she killed many of the saints of God, and she greatly enjoyed killing them).

4. (Revelation.18) The destruction of Babylon.

5. **God's saints are told to come out of her.**

6. She is destroyed in one day.

7. Saints in heaven praise God for her destruction (Revelation.19:1-6).

The marriage of the Lamb is announced
(Revelation 19:7-10)

The Lamb's wife, the church, has made herself ready (Revelation.19:7) She was arrayed in fine linen clean and white (the righteousness of the saints which was given to them by Jesus Christ) (Revlation.19:8).

Christ and His armies appear and fight the battle of Armageddon.
(Revelation.19:11-16)

1. Heaven opens (Revelation.19:11).

2. Jesus comes riding on a white horse (Revelation.19:11).

3. Jesus has eyes as a flame of fire, and on His head are many crowns. (Revelation.19:11-12).

4. Jesus has a vesture dipped in blood and His name is called **the Word of God** (Revelation.19:13).

5. The armies which are in heaven do follow Him (Revelation.19:14).

6. Out of His mouth comes a sharp two edge sword that He smites the nations with (Revelation.19:15).

7. Jesus Christ will rule them all with a rod of iron. (Revelation.19:15).

8. **The battle of Armageddon** (Revelation.19:17-21).

9. The kings and their armies gather to a place called Armageddon to fight against Jesus.

10. The beast and the false prophet are cast into the lake of fire.

11. The men who came to fight against the Lamb are slain.

This will end the time of the Tribulation Period.

The Millennium

The 1000 year reign of Christ
and His church upon the earth
Revelation.20:1-10

The Millennium

The 1000 year reign of Christ
and His church upon the earth
(Revelation.20:1-10)

satan bound for 1000 years

*(Revelation.20:1-3) And I saw an angel come down from heaven, having the key of the bottomless pit and a great chain in his hand. 2. And he laid hold on the dragon, that old serpent, which is the Devil, and Satan, and bound him **a thousand years**, 3. And cast him into the bottomless pit, and shut him up, and set a seal upon him, that he should deceive the nations no more, till **the thousand years** should be fulfilled*

The devil is not as tough as he thinks he is. He thinks that no one can handle him, not even God; however, to show satan (and people) how weak the devil really is, God sends an angel to bind him. The devil is not even powerful enough to stop just one angel from binding him and casting him into the bottomless pit. The devil will be seal there for 1000 years until God says he can be loosed. The devil really is not in control of anything. God has overall control of everything.

Saints rule with Christ For 1000 years

(Revelation.20:4-5) 4. **_And I saw thrones, and they sat upon them, and judgment was given unto them_**: *and I saw the souls of them that were beheaded for the witness of Jesus, and for the word of God, and which had not worshipped the beast, neither his image, neither had received his mark upon their foreheads, or in their hands;* **_and they lived and reigned with Christ a thousand years_**. *5. But the rest of the dead lived not again until the thousand years were finished. This is the first resurrection.*

1. Jesus Christ will set up an earthly kingdom where He shall rule with His saints for 1000 years. The word "Millennium" means 1000. The Millennium is a 1000 year period.

2. The saints of the Church Age shall rule with Jesus Christ during this time. Those saints will be in glorified bodies

3. The martyred Tribulation saints will be resurrected in glorified bodies and will also rule with Jesus during those 1000 years

4. Sinners who had not accepted the mark of the beast and made it through the Tribulation Period will be in the Millennium; however, they will not be rulers nor will they have glorified bodies. If they die without having accepted Jesus Christ as Lord and Savior, they will spend eternity in the lake of fire.

5. There will be people born in physical none glorified bodies during the Millennium. If they do not accept Jesus Christ as their Lord and Savior, they will die lost and will spend eternity in the lake of fire. Those

who become saved will eventually receive glorified bodies however it is unclear as to when they shall receive their glorified bodies.

6. Because verse 5 ends by saying "*This is the first resurrection*", many believe that the Rapture of the church will be at the end of the Tribulation Period instead of before the Tribulation Period. This is the verse they use to prove that. I would admonish you to embark upon a study for yourself until you become convinced in your heart of the time of the Rapture. Before, during, or after the Tribulation Period; one thing I do know is that it's all in the hands of Jesus Christ. I trust Him and I trust what He does and does not do.

The lion and lamb shall lay together

During this time the lion will lay down with the lamb because all animals will eat straw and not meat. There shall be a great change in people and animals during this time.

> *(Isaiah.11:6-9) 6. The wolf also shall dwell with the lamb, and the leopard shall lie down with the kid; and the calf and the young lion and the fatling together; and a little child shall lead them. 7. And the cow and the bear shall feed; their young ones shall lie down together: and the lion shall eat straw like the ox. 8. And the sucking child shall play on the hole of the asp, and the weaned child shall put his hand on the cockatrice' den. 9. They shall not hurt nor destroy in all my holy mountain: for the earth shall be full of the knowledge of the Lord, as the waters cover the sea.*

> *(Isaiah.65:20-25) 20. There shall be no more thence an infant of days, nor an old man that hath not filled his days: for the child shall die an hundred years old; but* **the sinner being an hundred years old shall be accursed**. *21. And they shall build houses, and inhabit them; and they shall plant vineyards, and eat the fruit of them. 22. They shall not build, and another inhabit; they shall not plant, and another eat: for as the days of a tree are the days of my people, and mine elect shall long enjoy the work of their hands. 23. They shall not labour in vain, nor bring forth for trouble; for they are the seed of the blessed of the Lord, and their offspring with them. 24. And it shall come to pass, that before they call, I will answer; and while they are yet speaking, I will hear. 25. The wolf and the lamb shall feed together, and the lion shall eat straw like the bullock: and dust shall be the serpent's meat. They shall not hurt nor destroy in all my holy mountain, saith the Lord.*

1. Although people will have long lives during this period, those who do not have glorified bodies will die; but not before they become 100 years old. Babies will be born during the Millennium but they will be born sinners in physical bodies (they will not have glorified bodies) and will need to accept Jesus Christ as their Lord and Savior before they die to become saved.

2. There will be unsaved people during this time. **Many sinners who did not accept the mark of the beast but was alive at the end of the Tribulation Period** will enter into the Millennium unsaved. If they do not accept Jesus as their Lord and Savior during the Millennium they will die sinners and will spend eternity in the lake of fire.

   *All sinners <u>**who received the mark of the beast**</u> during the Tribulation Period will be destroyed (killed) when Jesus Christ returns for the battle of Armageddon.*

3. People will work during the Millennium. They will build houses, plant vineyards and gardens, and do many other things.

4. People will pray, and God will answer their prayers.

5. Snakes (serpents) will eat dust. They will no longer be poisonous.

6. As you study the Holy Bible (especially the books of Isaiah and Ezekiel) you will learn much, much more about this time period.

Jesus and the nations

1. The earthly city of Jerusalem will be in the Millennium. The temple of God will be there and Jesus Christ will rule and reign from that temple. All animal sacrifices will cease. All will realize that Jesus Christ is the Lamb of God, and His sacrifice paid for all sins eternally.

2. There will be many different nations on earth at this time and the saints of Christ shall be ruling these nations.

3. The nations will come up to Jerusalem to worship and praise God and the Lamb Jesus Christ.

4. The devil and demons will not be on earth during the Millennium. The devil will be bound in the bottomless pit for 1000 years. I believe that demons will be bound in hell during this time. When men do wrong it will be because their hearts are not right and not because the devil and demons tempted them. It is only when one accepts Jesus Christ as their Lord and Savior that their hearts become right in the sight of God.

The devil loosed
For a short season

1. (Revelation.20:7-10) After 1000 years satan is loosed and goes forth and deceives the nations of Gog and Magog to go against the saints in war.

2. He will be able to deceive only those who did not accept Jesus Christ as their Lord and Savior.

3. Fire falls from heaven and destroys them.

4. (Revelation.20:10) satan is cast into the lake of fire where the beast and the false prophet are and is tormented forever and ever.

The Great White Throne Judgment
(Revelation.20:11-15)

11. And I saw a great white throne, and him that sat on it, from whose face the earth and the heaven fled away; and there was found no place for them.

*12. And I saw the dead, small and great, stand before God; and **the books** were opened: and another book was opened, which is **the book of life**: and the dead were judged out of those things which were written in the books, according to their works.*

13. And the sea gave up the dead which were in it; and death and hell delivered up the dead which were in them: and they were judged every man according to their works.

14. And death and hell were cast into the lake of fire. This is the second death.

15. And whosoever was not found written in the book of life was cast into the lake of fire.

1. The Lord Jesus Christ will be the eternal Judge on the Great White Throne (John.5:22).

2. Judgment will be according to "**the books**". "The books" probably contains all the deeds done by sinful men.

3. "**The book of life**" contains all the names of those who are saved because they have accepted the Messiah Jesus Christ as their Lord and Savior. All whose names are not written in "the book of life" will be cast into the lake of fire.

4. There will only be sinners at this Great White Throne Judgment.

5. The sea, death, hell, and the grave will give up the dead that are in them.

6. No sinner will escape the judgment of God at this Great White Throne Judgment.

7. Sinners will be judged according to the things they did on earth while they were physically alive.

8. I believe their level of eternal torment will be determined at this judgment.

9. All will know that God's judgment is according to truth and righteousness.

The Lake of Fire
(Revelation.20:14-15)

14. And death and hell were cast into the lake of fire. This is the second death.

15. And whosoever was not found written in the book of life was cast into the lake of fire.

1. None will be able to say it is unfair for them to be sentenced to the lake of fire. They will all know they rightly belong there.

2. The devil will be in the lake of fire.

3. The antichrist (the beast) will be in the lake of fire.

4. The false prophet will be in the lake of fire.

5. Death and hell will be in the lake of fire.

6. All sinners will be in the lake of fire.

7. The lake of fire will be a place of eternal torment (Revelation.14:10-11).

Eternity Future

Revelation.21-22

Revelation.21:1-5

1. And I saw a new heaven and a new earth: for the first heaven and the first earth were passed away; and there was no more sea.

2. And I John saw the holy city, new Jerusalem, coming down from God out of heaven, prepared as a bride adorned for her husband.

3. And I heard a great voice out of heaven saying, Behold, the tabernacle of God is with men, and he will dwell with them, and they shall be his people, and God himself shall be with them, and be their God.

4. And God shall wipe away all tears from their eyes; and there shall be no more death, neither sorrow, nor crying, neither shall there be any more pain: for the former things are passed away.

5. And he that sat upon the throne said, Behold, I make all things new. And he said unto me, Write: for these words are true and faithful.

Revelation.22:1-5

1. And he shewed me a pure river of water of life, clear as crystal, proceeding out of the throne of God and of the Lamb.

2. In the midst of the street of it, and on either side of the river, was there the tree of life, which bare twelve manner of fruits, and yielded her fruit every month: and the leaves of the tree were for the healing of the nations.

3. And there shall be no more curse: but the throne of God and of the Lamb shall be in it; and his servants shall serve him:

4. And they shall see his face; and his name shall be in their foreheads.

5. And there shall be no night there; and they need no candle, neither light of the sun; for the Lord God giveth them light: and they shall reign for ever and ever.

Eternity Future

A. There will be a new heaven and a new earth.

B. God will dwell with men and shall be their God.

C. God shall wipe away all tears from their eyes.

D. There shall be no more death, neither sorrow, nor crying, neither shall there be any more pain: for the former things are passed away.

E. The Holy City **New Jerusalem** will come down from heaven to earth. In the New Jerusalem there will be:

   1. Gates of pearls.
   2. Streets of gold.
   3. The river of life.
   4. The tree of life.
   5. The throne of God and of the Lamb.
   6. Some believe this New Jerusalem will not touch the earth but will be suspended above the earth.
   7. Much, much, much, more.

H. This time period will never end.

Those who will live in
Eternity Future with God

A. Those of the Old Testament who believed in the coming Messiah. These are the saints of the Old Testament. *(Job.19:25)* *[25]For I know that my redeemer liveth, and that he shall stand at the latter day upon the earth: [26]And though after my skin worms destroy this body, yet in my flesh shall I see God: [27]Whom I shall see for myself, and mine eyes shall behold, and not another; though my reins be consumed within me.*

B. The way it showed that these Old Testament saints were looking for the coming Messiah was that they truly loved the Lord and tried to obey His Law, when God gave them the Law through Moses, (although they fail at keeping all of the Law of God, they did try). *(Deuteronomy.33:2-4)* ²*And he said, The LORD came from Sinai, and rose up from Seir unto them; he shined forth from mount Paran, and he came with ten thousands of saints: from his right hand went a fiery law for them.* ³*Yea, he loved the people; all his saints are in thy hand: and they sat down at thy feet; every one shall receive of thy words.* ⁴*Moses commanded us a law, even the inheritance of the congregation of Jacob.*

C. All those of the New Testament who by faith have accepted Jesus Christ as their Lord and Savior *(Romans.10:9-10)* ⁹*That if thou shalt confess with thy mouth the Lord Jesus, and shalt believe in thine heart that God hath raised him from the dead, thou shalt be saved.* ¹⁰*For with the heart man believeth unto righteousness; and with the mouth confession is made unto salvation.*

D. All those of the Tribulation Period who accepted Jesus Christ as their Lord and Savior. *(Revelation.7:13-17)* ¹³*And one of the elders answered, saying unto me, What are these which are arrayed in white robes? and whence came they?* ¹⁴*And I said unto him, Sir, thou knowest. And he said to me, These are they which came out of great tribulation, and have washed their robes, and made them white in the blood of the Lamb.* ¹⁵*Therefore are they before the throne of God, and serve him day and night in his temple: and he that sitteth on the throne shall dwell among them.* ¹⁶*They shall hunger no more, neither thirst any more; neither shall the sun light on them, nor any heat.* ¹⁷*For the Lamb which is in the midst of the throne shall feed them, and shall lead them unto living fountains of waters: and God shall wipe away all tears from their eyes.*

E. All those of the Millennium who accept Jesus Christ as their Lord and Savior. *(Revelation.20:4-9)* ⁴*And I saw thrones, and they sat upon them, and judgment was given unto them: and I saw the souls of them that were beheaded for the witness of Jesus, and for the word of God, and which had not worshipped the beast, neither his image, neither had received his mark* *upon their foreheads, or in their hands; and they lived and reigned with Christ a thousand years. ⁵But the rest of the dead lived not again until the thousand years were finished. This is the first resurrection. ⁶Blessed and holy is he that hath part in the first resurrection: on such the second death hath no power, but they shall be priests of God and of Christ, and shall reign with him a thousand years. ⁷And when the thousand years are expired, Satan shall be loosed out of his prison, ⁸And shall go out to deceive the nations which are in the four quarters of the earth, Gog and Magog, to gather them together to battle: the number of whom is as the sand of the sea. ⁹And they went up on the breadth of the earth,* **and compassed the camp of the saints** *about, and the beloved city: and fire came down from God out of heaven, and devoured them.*

F. All whose names are written in the Book of Life *(Revelation.20:15) ¹⁵And whosoever was not found written in the book of life was cast into the lake of fire.*

G. All the heavenly host. *(Revelation.7:11-12) ¹¹And all the angels stood round about the throne, and about the elders and the four beasts, and fell before the throne on their faces, and worshipped God, ¹²Saying, Amen: Blessing, and glory, and wisdom, and thanksgiving, and honour, and power, and might, be unto our God for ever and ever. Amen.*

Overview of God's dealings with mankind

How God deals with mankind
From eternity past to eternity future

In this portion of our study we are going to discuss seven ways God deals with man from **Eternity Past** to **Eternity Future**. We will start with Eternity Past because He started dealing with man even before He created man (Ephesians.1:4). **While God deals with mankind in different ways; He Himself never changes.** Regardless of how He deals with man He is still love, holy, merciful, kind, the eternal Judge, Omnipotent (Almighty), Omniscient (All-knowing), Omnipresent (ever present), etc.

The term Theologians use to describe how God deals with mankind for a certain period of time is **"Dispensations"**. *However the divisions we are using are not dispensations as theologians classifies them. Our divisions are just an overview of how God deals with mankind. Our divisions are:*

1. **Eternity past.** The time before the physical creation.

2. **Patriarchs:** Patriarchs are chief men and women of a certain time period.

3. **The Law and the prophets:** God dealt with man through **His laws and prophets.**

4. **Grace:** "**God's un-merited favor**." God offering men His salvation, love, and blessings although they could never deserve them, earn them, or pay for them.

5. **Tribulation Period (the time of wrath of God):** A seven-year time period when God will deal with man through His wrath, and will allow the antichrist to rule the world.

6. **Millennium:** God will deal with mankind through allowing saints to rule with Jesus Christ on earth for a Millennium (1000 years).

7. **Eternity future.** The time after the Millennium when saints will forever be with God.

Regardless of how God deals with man, He is still love, holy, just, slow to anger, full of grace, and full of compassion. **God's methods of dealing with mankind may change, but His attributes will never change**. Below is a chart of how we, and others, view what God is doing from Eternity Past to Eternity Future. **Our chart is for our study only**. However, we will first show you the dispensations other theologians use.

Some Theologians	Other Theologians	For our study
1. Innocence	1. Innocence	1. Eternity Past
2. Human knowledge	2. Human knowledge	2. Patriarchs
3. Human government	3. Human government	3. Law and Prophets
4. The Law and the prophets	4. Promise	4. Grace (Church age)
5. The Dispensation of grace	5. The Law and the prophets	5. Tribulation Period
6. The Tribulation Period	6. The Dispensation of grace	6. Millennium
7. The Millennium	7. The Millennium	7. Eternity Future

From eternity past to eternity future

Eternity Past	The Patriarchs Old Testament	The Law and the Prophets Old Testament	The Church Age New Testament
Creation of the third heaven where God dwells Creation of angels and all the heavenly host Fall of satan and 1/3rd of the angels God made hell and the lake of fire for the devil and his angels Preparation for creation of mankind and the redemption of mankind through Jesus Christ (see *Ephesians 1:4*)	**2000 years** Creation as found in Genesis:1-2 **Innocence** the time before men sinned **The fall** man sinned in the Garden and became sinners **Human knowledge** God now had to deal with man through human knowledge **Human Government** is established **Promise Patriarch are** (chief men and women like Noah, Abraham, Sarah, Isaac, Jacob, Job, Tamar, Joseph)	**2000 years** Moses and the Law All the events of the Old Testament from Moses to Christ **The birth** and earthly ministry of Jesus Christ. (Jesus ministered under the O.T. Law) The **death** of Jesus on the Cross **Resurrection** and **ascension** of Jesus Christ In the Holy Bible the events of the gospels are included in the New Testament; however, the New Testament really began on the day of Pentecost when the Holy Spirit came to indwell saints.	**2000 years** The Holy Spirit coming down to indwell saints All the events in the book of Acts The Epistles All of the events concerning the church **The Rapture** of the church (*1 Thessalonians 4:15-17*) Many believe that the Rapture of the church will signal the end of the Church Age of **the Dispensation of Grace** **The Church Age** is called 1. The Church Age 2. The Dispensation of Grace 3. The **Times of the Gentiles**. 4. The New Testament

Tribulation Period The time of God's wrath New Testament	**The Millennium** New Testament	**Eternity Future**
7 years The antichrist makes a **7-year peace treaty** between Israel and her enemies the 7 seals including 1. the 4 horsemen 2. the 7 trumpets 3. The 3 woes 4. The 2 witnesses satan kicked out of heaven The beast out of the sea The beast out of the earth The mark of the beast 666 The destruction of Mystery Babylon The battle of **Armageddon** The devil bound in the bottomless pit	**1000 years** satan bound for 1000 years Saints ruling on earth with Jesus The devil loosed after 1000 years The devil deceives Gog and Magog to fight against the saints God sends down fire to destroy them The devil is cast into The Lake of Fire The Great White Throne Judgment seat of God Almighty The second death	**Forever and forever** The new heaven and the new earth The New Jerusalem The tree of life The river of life All of the never ending events in Eternity Future

Eternity Past
(Preparation time)

Eternity Past refers to the time **before** creation as found in the book of Genesis chapters one and two. All of the events that occurred before the physical creation are all included in a time period I refer to as **"Eternity Past."**

A. During Eternity Past God created the 3rd heaven where He and the angels dwell (*2nd Corinthians 12:2*).

B. During Eternity Past, God created the angels and all the heavenly creatures *(Revelation.10:6)*.

C. During Eternity Past, lucifer rebelled against God and deceived 1/3rd of the angels to join in with him in his rebellion. They were all expelled from heaven (kicked out of heaven). God had Michael the Archangel to kick lucifer and his fallen angels out of heaven. (*Isaiah 14:12-15, Ezekiel 28:14-17, Revelation 12:7-9*) Many believe that Revelation. 12:7-9 speaks of what happened in Eternity Past as well as what will happen during the Tribulation Period when he will no longer be allowed to access heaven.

D. After being kicked out of heaven lucifer (light bearer) became satan (adversary) the devil (deceiver). (*Isaiah. 14:12 Revelation 12:9*).

E. After being kicked out of heaven, the fallen angels (those angels who sided in with lucifer) became demons (also called devils and unclean spirits).

F. After being kicked out of heaven, they were eternally locked into their decision of being against God. Angels will always be angels who love God, obey God and serve God. Demons will always be demons who are against God and the things of God.

G. During Eternity Past, God created a place called hell (and The Lake of Fire) to eventually be the eternal place of torment for the devil, demons, and all who sides in with them by rejecting Jesus Christ as their Lord and Savior. (*Matthew 25:41*). Sinners go to hell when they die until the Day of Judgment. After the Day of Judgment, they and hell itself will be cast into the Lake of Fire (Revelation.20:11-15).

H. After kicking lucifer and his fallen angels out of heaven, God then started preparing for men whom He would eventually create and redeem (*See Ephesians 1:4:* 1st *Peter 1:19-20*). Men were in the heart, mind, and eternal plan of God even before He created them. Because God started preparing for men even before He made man, I often refer to Eternity Past as **a time of preparation**.

> *(1st Peter 1:19-20) 19. But with the precious blood of Christ, as of a lamb without blemish and without spot: 20. Who verily* **<u>was foreordained before the foundation of the world</u>**, *but was manifest in these last times for you.*

While we use the phrase "**Eternity Past**"; eternity actually has no beginning or ending. God started time for man's sake. He started it at the creation and He will end it after the Millennium. Time as we now know it will one day cease to be. That is why one day is as a thousand years and a thousand years as one day to God. To God, it's all a part of eternity.

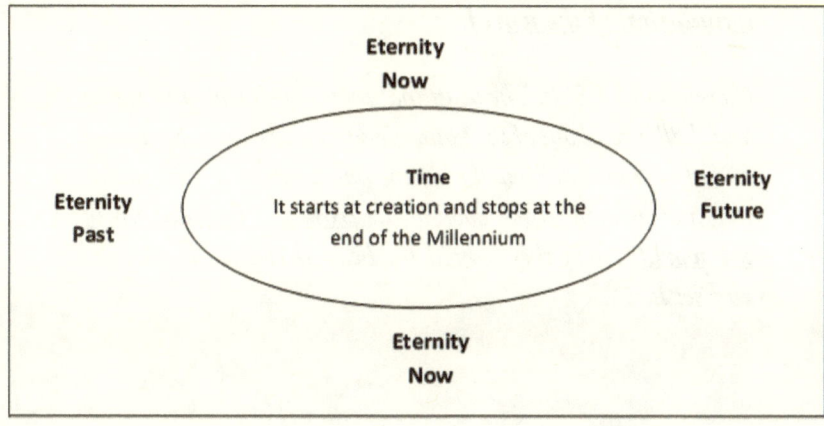

> *(Revelation 10:5-6) 5. And the angel which I saw stand upon the sea and upon the earth lifted up his hand to heaven, 6. And sware by him that liveth for ever and ever, who created heaven, and the things that therein are, and the earth, and the things that therein are, and the sea, and the things which are therein,* ***that there should be time no longer:***

God set time in motion for man's benefit. Men reference things according to time, and men understand things according to time. God functions inside of time and God functions outside of time. Men make plans for time while God makes plans for eternity. One-day God will cause time to cease and be no more.

<u>In Eternity Past God predestined and foreordained the redemptive work of Jesus Christ. In Eternity Past God knew who would choose Him by choosing Jesus as their Lord and Savior; thus He wrote their names down in the book of life. He did it even before He created them or created this world.</u>

> *(Ephesians 1:4) 4. According as he hath chosen us in him* ***before the foundation of the world****, that we should be holy and without blame before him in love.*

> *(Hebrews 4:3) 3. For we which have believed do enter into rest, as he said, As I have sworn in my wrath, if they shall enter into my rest: although the works were finished* ***from the foundation of the world****.*

> *(Revelation 17:8) 8. The beast that thou sawest was, and is not; and shall ascend out of the bottomless pit, and go into perdition: and they that dwell on the earth shall wonder, whose names were not written in the book of life* ***from the foundation of the world****, when they behold the beast that was, and is not, and yet is.*

Times of the Patriarchs
The first 2000 years of the Old Testament

Our first division was **eternity past, the time of preparation.** Our second division is **the Times of the Patriarchs**. The time period of the Patriarchs began at the physical creation as recorded in the book of Genesis. It lasted until the coming of Moses and the Law.

Major Events of the Old Testament
Times of the Patriarchs includes

A. **Creation of physical things:** This is the time period when God created the heavens and the earth. The heavens spoken of in Genesis are outer space and earth's atmosphere. He is not speaking of the Third Heaven where He and angels dwell. (*2nd Corinthians.12:2*) The Third Heaven was created in eternity past.

B. <u>*Innocence:*</u> The time of **innocence** is the time from the creation of Adam and Eve up until they sin by eating of the fruit from the Tree of the Knowledge of Good and Evil. Some call this time period **the Dispensation of Innocence** because they were without sin.

   1. During innocence, God could deal with mankind as clean sinless beings.

   2. During innocence, God could fellowship and commune with man One on one. He came down in the cool of the day to fellowship and commune with Adam and Eve.

C. **The fall: The time of Human knowledge:** This is when Adam and Eve ate from the forbidden tree and thus became **sinners**. Some call this **The Dispensation of Human knowledge;** because mankind now possessed physical sinful human knowledge.

1. God now had to deal with men as **sinful beings**.

2. God now had to deal with men who now possesses a **sin nature**.

3. God now had to deal with men through the fact that sin was now **being passed on to every generation** thereafter.

4. God had to deal with men as **being spiritually separated** from Him. There was no more One on one fellowship and communion between God and man.

5. God now had to deal with man through **animal sacrifices**.

    i. The blood of specific animals now had to be shed to cover man's sins.

    ii. Because animals had not sinned, **certain animals**' blood could cover sin, but never wash it away. The blood of animals could not eternally cleanse the one who has sinned, and could never make them holy or righteous in the sight of God. **Only the blood of Jesus Christ could do that**.

    iii. The blood of sinful men was too polluted and contaminated with sin to be used for sacrifices for sin. That is why God **hated** the human sacrifices of pagan nations.

    iv. When it got to the time when too much sin had entered into the world, the blood of animals could no longer cover it; thus, God found no more pleasure in sacrifice and offerings of animals for sin. He then had to send His Son Jesus Christ into the world to shed His blood as the perfect sacrifice to totally wash away sin. (*Hebrews 10:6-9*) Jesus is the Lamb of God that takes away the sins of the world (John.1:29).

6. God now had to deal with man through **priests** who would now intercede between God and man until Jesus came.

7. ***Human knowledge*:** God now had to deal with man through human physical knowledge.

8. ***Human governments*:** God now had to deal with men through human governments which men would eventually set up. God wanted a Theocracy (God ruled kingdom) but men established men ruling kingdoms.

D. **The time of the Patriarchs,** was a time period when God dealt with certain men and women called **patriarchs** or "**chief fathers, or chief mothers;**" and revealed His will and ways to them. These chief fathers (patriarchs) included such men and women as Seth, Enoch, Methuselah, Noah, Abraham, Sarah, Lot, (**Melchizedek**), Isaac, Jacob, Tamar, Job (*Genesis.46:13*), Joseph, and others.

E. ***Promise:*** During the times of the patriarchs God promised to give the Promised Land of Canaan that flows with milk and honey to Abraham, and to his descendants that Abraham would have through the promised child **Isaac**, and then through **Jacob** (Israel) and then through **Jacob's twelve sons**.

F. During the times of the Patriarchs, the children of Israel went down to Egypt and became a great nation there.

1. It was seventy of them which went down to Egypt in the days of Joseph; however, those seventy eventually grew into a mighty nation called the Jews and/or the Children of Israel (*Exodus 1:5*). They eventually became slaves to the Egyptians.

2. God, through Moses, delivered the children of Israel out of Egyptian bondage.

3. Once God delivered them out of Egyptian bondage, He gave them His laws. Instead of dealing with them through the patriarchs, God would now deal with them through **His Laws and prophets.**

G. The coming of Moses to deliver the children of Israel out of Egyptian bondage ended the dispensation of the patriarchs and began **the Dispensation of the Law and the prophets**.

H. Many believe that from creation up to the coming of Moses and the law was **2000 years**.

The Old Testament times of The Law and the prophets
The second 2000 years of the Old Testament
(also called the Dispensation of Law)

The time from Moses and the Law, up to the time when Jesus Christ ascended up into heaven and sent back the Holy Spirit on the day of Pentecost, is called the time of **the Dispensation of the Law and the Prophets.** It is believed to have lasted 2000 years. God dealt with man and made His will and ways known to men through the laws He gave through Moses. He also dealt with men through the prophets He raised up to speak for Him.

Major things that happened during the Dispensation of the Law and prophets

A. God delivered Israel out of Egyptian bondage.

B. God gave Israel the **Law** through Moses.

C. There were 40 years of wondering in the wilderness.

D. After 40 years of wondering in the wilderness, Israel entered into the **Promised Land** and possessed it.

E. The times of the **judges** take place.

F. The times of the **kings** take place.

G. The Nation of Israel divided into **two nations.** These two nations were **Israel** to the north (10 tribes) and **Judah** to the south (2 tribes which were Judah and Benjamin).

H. **Israel** goes into **Assyrian captivity** because of their sins and idolatry.

I. **Judah** later goes into **Babylonian captivity** for **70** years because of their sins and idolatry.

J. Judah returned back to Jerusalem after 70 years and rebuilt the walls, the temple and the city.

K. **400** years of silence where it is believed that God did not speak to anyone upon the earth.

L. The virgin birth, life, death, resurrection, and ascension of **Jesus Christ** takes place. Although the life and ministry of Christ is recorded in the New Testament, it was actually performed under the Old Testament Dispensation of Law.

M. The time period of **the Law and the Prophets** is believed to have lasted for 2000 years.

There are many, many more events that transpired during this time of the Dispensation of Law than what we have mentioned here. As you daily read and meditate upon the written Word of God you will learn of these events and of the people involved in these events. As you read of them, ask God to reveal to you how these people and events relate to His Son Jesus Christ and the redemptive work He accomplished on the Cross.

The New Testament
The Church Age;
The Dispensation of Grace;
The times of the Gentiles
(2000 years)

The Church Age began on the day of Pentecost when Jesus Christ the risen Savior sent the Holy Spirit to indwell believers (*Acts 2:1-4*), and will continue up until the Rapture of the Church (*1 Thessalonians 4:15-17*). It is believed by many theologians that the Church Age will last for **2000 years**. When it ends, the Tribulation Period will eventually begin. Some believe it is not the Rapture but the signing of a seven-year peace treaty which starts the Tribulation Period.

The Church Age,
The dispensation of grace
The times of the gentiles

A. **The Church Age:** A time when God is calling out a people (both Jews and Gentiles) to be a part of His eternal family. In this dispensation God's chosen people is the church (1st Peter.2:9) however He has not rescinded His promises concerning Jews: He has only postponed them until the time of the end. And because Jews are now back in their land, the time of the end is upon us now.

B. **The Dispensation of Grace:** The Church Age is also called the Dispensation of Grace. It is call that because God is dealing with men through His Grace because of the redemptive work of His Son Jesus Christ on the Cross.

1. **Grace** is God offering men His salvation, love, and blessings although they could never deserve them, earn them, or pay for them. That's called, "**God's un-merited favor.**" Men enter into God's grace by accepting Jesus Christ as their Lord and Savior.

2. Instead of dealing with men through their sinfulness, God deals with men through **His holiness and righteousness** that He gives to all who by faith accepts Jesus Christ as their Lord and Savior.

C. **The times of the Gentiles:** The Church Age is also called the times of the Gentiles because God's major focus has shifted from the Jews in the Old Testament, to the gentiles (and Jews) during this New Testament time. God is calling out a people from all races and nations to become a part of His eternal family and kingdom through His Son Jesus Christ.

D. **The Rapture of the Church:** The expected prophetic event which will signal the end of the Church Age is **the Rapture of the Church.** (*see 1st Thessalonians 4:16-17*)

1. Jesus will descend from heaven with a shout, and with the voice of the Archangel and with the trump of God. However He will stop in the clouds of the air and will not touch the ground at this time.

2. Those who died believing in Jesus Christ will rise from the dead in glorified bodies.

3. Those who are alive when Jesus Christ returns will instantly be changed into glorified bodies.

4. All saints will then ascend into the clouds of the air to meet with Jesus Christ and will forever be with Jesus Christ.

5. This is called **the Rapture of the church**.

6. This will happen in a moment and in a twinkling of an eye.

Different theologians have different views as to when the Rapture will occur. There are three major views of when it will occur. These three different views are listed and discussed below.

E. **Different views of when the Rapture will occur:**

   1. **Pre-Trib**: Many believe the Rapture of the church will happen before the Tribulation Period begins. This is call the Pre-trib Rapture. (1st Thessalonians.4:15-17).

   2. **Mid-trib**: Many believe the Rapture of the church will happen in the middle of the Tribulation Period. This is called Mid-trib Rapture. (Revelation.14:14-16).

   3. **Post-Trib**: Many believe the Rapture of the church will happen at the end of the Tribulation Period. This is called Post-trib Rapture. (Revelation.20:5-6).

Study the scriptures for yourself while asking God the Father, in Jesus' name, to reveal to you, which view of when the Rapture occurs, does He desires you to hold to.

Regardless of the view of the Rapture you hold; it will not change the sequence of end time events.

The Tribulation Period (7 years)
The time of the wrath of God and the judgment of God
The times of Jacob's trouble
The times of the devil and demons
The time of the antichrist
The Great Tribulation Period

This time period will begin after **the Rapture of the church**, and at the time when the antichrist will make **a seven year peace treaty** between Israel and her enemies (although there may be a brief time span of weeks, months or years after the Rapture before the treaty is made). The Tribulation Period will last 7 years and will include all of the events in the **Book of Revelation chapter 6 through chapter 20:1-2**. The second 3 ½ years of this seven-year period will be called "**The Great Tribulation Period.**" (*Matthew 24:21*)

Major events during the Tribulation Period

A. Israel would have already become a mighty independent nation.

B. There will be a resurgence of the Old Roman Empire (or a governmental system which will resemble the old Roman Empire of the past). This empire will eventually be transformed into the antichrist world ruling kingdom.

C. It is my belief that the church would have already been Raptured into heaven; although not all hold this belief.

D. The Tribulation Period will become the worst times this world has ever experienced, and will only get worse and worse until the return of Jesus Christ to establish the Millennium.

E. There will be wars and rumors of wars, false Christ's shall come, and the love of many will grow cold. Iniquity shall abound and many horrific events shall occur.

F. The Jews will rebuild their temple and return to animal sacrifices. This will show that many Jews still reject Jesus Christ as their Savior and as the perfect and only sacrifice for all sins.

G. Many nations of the world will come against Israel to battle against her.

H. The antichrist will make a seven-year peace treaty between Israel and her enemies. However; He will break that peace treaty after 3 ½ years.

I. The seven seals (including the four horsemen).

J. The sealing of the 144,000 Jewish servants of God.

K. A time of great and untold national disasters (great earthquakes, hailstones mixed with fire, the sun, moon, and stars not shining, the moon turning to blood, etc.).

L. The seven trumpets (demonic spirits coming to torment and/or kill men).

M. The three woes.

N. The two witnesses.

O. satan kicked out of heaven.

P. The beast out of the sea.

Q. The beast out of the earth.

R. The mark of the beast 666.

S. The seven angels of Revelation chapter 14.

T. mYSTERY Babylon.

U. The destruction of Babylon.

V. The coming of Jesus Christ with His church to fight the battle of Armageddon. The antichrist and the false prophet will be cast into the Lake of Fire.

W. The devil bound in the bottomless pit for 1000 years.

X. And much, much, more as revealed in the book of Revelation.

The Millennium

This is the time period after the Tribulation Period ends and satan is bound for 1000 years in the bottomless pit. It will end at the Great White Throne Judgment.

A. Saints will rule with Christ on earth for 1000 years. The word "**millennium**" means "1000".

B. After the 1000 years are up, satan will be loosed out of the bottomless pit and then go about to deceive Gog and Magog into fighting against the saints of God. God will rain down fire from heaven and destroy them.

C. The devil will be cast into The Lake of Fire.

D. **The Great White Throne Judgment** will occur, and all whose names are not found written in **the Book of Life** will be cast into **The Lake of Fire** (*Revelation 20:1-15*). Being cast into the Lake of Fire is called, "**The second death.**"

Eternity Future

Revelation 21-22 describes some of the events that will transpire during **Eternity Future**.

1. There will be a new heaven and a new earth.

2. God will dwell with men and shall be their God.

3. God shall wipe away all tears from their eyes.

4. There shall be no more death, neither sorrow, nor crying, neither shall there be any more pain: for the former things are passed away.

5. The Holy City **New Jerusalem** will come down from heaven to earth. In the New Jerusalem there will be:

    A. Gates of pearls.

    B. Streets of gold.

    C. The river of life.

    D. The tree of life.

    E. The throne of God and of the Lamb.

    F. Some believe this New Jerusalem will not touch the earth but will be suspended above the earth.

6. This time period will never end.

The book of Revelation deals with the ending of the Church Age through Eternity Future

1. Chapters 1-3 deals with the **Church Age**.

2. Chapters 4-5 deals with **the church in heaven** during the Tribulation Period.

3. Chapters 6-19 deals with the **Tribulation Period**.

4. Chapter 20 deals with the **Millennium**.

5. Chapters 21-22 deals with **Eternity Future**.

Jesus is LORD

www.ingramcontent.com/pod-product-compliance
Lightning Source LLC
Chambersburg PA
CBHW020519080526
44583CB00013B/663